The Sermon
on the Mount
According to Vedanta

The Sermon on the Mount According to Vedanta

BY SWAMI PRABHAVANANDA

Vedanta Press

Hollywood, California 90068

International Standard Book Number 0-87481-002-7
Library of Congress Catalog Card Number 64-8660
First published in the United States in 1964
5   6   7   8   9   10

Those who wish to learn in greater detail about the teachings contained in this book are invited to write to The secretary, Vedanta Society of Southern California, 1946 Vedanta Place, Hollywood, California 90068.

CONTENTS

Foreword by Henry James Forman

Introduction

FOREWORD

A BOOK on the Sermon on the Mount, which is the very heart of the Christian teaching, should be no novelty in a Christian community. But when that book is written by a Hindu swami, a follower of Vedanta and the gospel of Sri Ramakrishna, a book, moreover, not only interpreting, but extolling the Sermon as though it were a scripture of his own, that certainly is, to say the least, unusual.

Beautiful as this interpretation is in itself, it is presented by Swami Prabhavananda not as a far-off, scarcely attainable ideal, which is the way most occidentals read the Sermon, but as a practical programme of daily living and conduct. So clear is the Swami's reading of this great scripture, that many a Christian by means of it will discover a simpler approach to the teaching of his Master, more direct than any he had found heretofore.

Vedanta teaches that man's real nature is divine and that the chief, the only real goal of human life is to unfold and manifest that Divinity. To us the Sermon is a counsel of perfection. To the Vedantist, whose sole aim is God-realization, that is nothing strange. The sannyasin of the Ramakrishna Order, to which Swami Prabhavananda belongs, follows the way of perfection every day of his life. Every day in his meditation he prays that he may overcome the sense of ego, that he may abstain from fault-finding and criticism of others, and that he may acquire love and sympathy for all. The Vedantist cannot sit down to meditate until he clears his mind of all hatreds and resentments. The literature of the Ramakrishna Order, as for instance the Gospel of Sri Ramakrishna, the writings of Swami Vivekananda, and that priceless little book by Swami Prabhavananda, *The Eternal Companion*, all are filled with teachings similar to those of the Sermon and other parts of our Bible.

THE SERMON ON THE MOUNT ACCORDING TO VEDANTA

In the book of Exodus we read that when Moses came down from the mount, 'Moses wist not that the skin of his face shone'. Swami Prabhavananda in this volume tells of seeing one of his elders, a direct disciple of Sri Ramakrishna, so transfigured. A light emanated from his whole body. Not only did Swami Prabhavananda see it, but crowds of people in a temple lane where it occurred, fell back in amazement and made way as the illumined holy man walked in complete absorption in the thought of God.

Phenomena of that order are not confined to scriptures dating hundreds and thousands of years back. They can and do occur today. Religion is a continuing fact in human life. The prescriptions of the Sermon on the Mount can be and are lived today. It depends upon the spirit in which they are accepted. Swami Prabhavananda and his fellow-Vedantists accept them realistically. That is probably the reason that people of various creeds and Christian sects, who come to the lectures on Vedanta, often find that their own creed appears suddenly brighter and more luminous, and their understanding of it attains a deeper penetration.

Vedanta, briefly, comes to the West not to supplant any religion, but to bring a more tangible spirituality to those who seek it. Its goal is not to proselytize, but to help man realize the divinity within him. In that it claims, not without reason, to be the most practical of religious philosophies. And that practicality is what Swami Prabhavananda successfully conveys in his remarkably fine and lucid interpretation of the Sermon on the Mount.

HENRY JAMES FORMAN

ACKNOWLEDGMENTS

ACKNOWLEDGMENTS are due to a number of publishers for permission to reprint selections from their books: to Advaita Ashrama, Mayavati, India, for passages from *The Complete Works of Swami Vivekananda;* to Methuen & Company, Ltd., London, for a passage from *The Confessions of Jacob Boehme,* compiled and edited by W. Scott Palmer; to the Society for Promoting Christian Knowledge, London, for passages from *The Way of a Pilgrim* and *The Pilgrim Continues His Way,* translated from the Russian by R. M. French; and to the Vedanta Society of Southern California for passages from the following works: *How to Know God, the Yoga Aphorisms of Patanjali,* translated with a new commentary by Swami Prabhavananda and Christopher Isherwood; *The Song of God: Bhagavad-Gita,* translated by Prabhavananda and Isherwood; *The Upanishads,* translated by Prabhavananda and Frederick Manchester; *The Wisdom of God (Srimad Bhagavatam),* translated by Prabhavananda.

Selections from Sri Ramakrishna's life and teachings are principally from *Sri Sri Ramakrishna Lilaprasanga,* by Swami Saradananda, and *Sri Sri Ramakrishna Kathamrita,* by M.

The lectures upon which this book is based were given by the author at the Hollywood and Santa Barbara temples of the Vedanta Society of Southern California. Some portions of the material have appeared in the magazine *Vedanta and the West* and in an anthology, *Vedanta for the Western World,* edited by Christopher Isherwood.

I would like to thank Henry James Forman for writing the preface. I am indebted to Pravrajika Anandaprana for editing the manuscript and giving the book its present form, and to Benjamin Saltman for editorial assistance.

S.P.

INTRODUCTION

THIS book is based on lectures I have given on the Sermon on the Mount. The lectures have been revised and expanded to cover teachings not previously commented upon. To me, the Sermon on the Mount represents the essence of Christ's gospel; and it is printed here in its entirety, as it is set down, so that Christ's words may be read in sequence and the unity of his message may be clearly seen.

I am not a Christian, I am not a theologian, I have not read the Bible interpretations of the great Christian scholars. I have studied the New Testament as I have studied the scriptures of my own religion, Vedanta. Vedanta, which evolved from the Vedas, the most ancient of Hindu scriptures, teaches that all religions are true inasmuch as they lead to one and the same goal—God-realization. My religion therefore accepts and reveres all the great prophets, spiritual teachers, and aspects of the Godhead worshipped in different faiths, considering them to be manifestations of one underlying truth.

As a young monk, I dwelt in close association with most of the monastic disciples of Sri Ramakrishna, the founder of the order to which I belong. These holy men lived in the consciousness of God and taught us the methods by which one may reach the ultimate and blessed state of mystic union—samadhi, as it is called in Vedanta. From what I have seen in these holy men, and from whatever understanding I have gained sitting at their feet, I have tried to approach the teachings of Christ. This is why I have often turned to the words of Sri Ramakrishna and his disciples to help explain the truths of the Sermon on the Mount.

One of these disciples of Sri Ramakrishna was my master, Swami Brahmananda. Although he was not a student of the Bible, from his own spiritual experience he taught in much the same way as Christ did, and often used almost the same words. My master had seen Christ in spiritual vision, and celebrated Christmas every year by offering special worship to Jesus, a custom which has been observed in all the monasteries of the Ramakrishna Order to the present day. On these occasions fruit, bread, and cake are offered in our Hindu way. Often there is a lecture on Christ; or the story of the Nativity or the Sermon on the Mount is read.

One of these Christmas celebrations, the first I ever attended, had great bearing on what Christ means to me. It took place in 1914 at Belur Math near Calcutta, where the headquarters of our order are situated. I had joined the monastery just a few days before. On Christmas Eve, we gathered before an altar on which a picture of the Madonna and Child had been placed. One of the senior monks performed worship with offerings of flowers, incense, and food. Many of Sri Ramakrishna's disciples attended the service, among them my master, who was the president of our order. While we were seated in silence, my master said: 'Meditate on Christ within, and feel his living presence.' An intense spiritual atmosphere pervaded the worship hall. Our minds were lifted up, and we felt ourselves transported into another consciousness. For the first time I realized that Christ was as much our own as Krishna, Buddha, and other great illumined teachers whom we revered. As a Hindu, I was taught from childhood to respect all religious ideals, to recognize the same divine inspiration in all the different faiths. Thus Christ as a manifest expression of divinity I could never have considered foreign. But for a living and personal experience of him I needed the tangible heightening of consciousness resulting from the worship on that memorable Christmas Eve.

An intimate spiritual connection between Christ and my monastic order has existed for many years, beginning with its founder, Sri Ramakrishna, who was accorded divine worship

during his lifetime and since his passing away in 1886 has received growing recognition in India as an incarnation of God.
Of the many saints and illumined teachers in the history
of Vedanta, Sri Ramakrishna expressed in his life to a greater
degree than any other teacher the idea of religious universality
and harmony. Not only did he undergo the disciplines of
divergent sects within Hinduism but those of Mohammedanism
and Christianity as well. Through each religious path he
achieved the supreme realization of God, and thus was able to
proclaim with the authority of direct experience: 'So many
religions, so many paths to reach one and the same goal.'

It was about 1874 that Sri Ramakrishna interested himself
actively in Christianity. A devotee who used to visit the
Master at the Dakshineswar temple garden near Calcutta
would explain the Bible to him in Bengali. One day, while Sri
Ramakrishna was seated in the drawing-room of another devotee's home, he saw a picture of the Madonna and Child.
Absorbed in contemplation of this picture, he saw it suddenly
become living and effulgent. An ecstatic love for Christ filled
Sri Ramakrishna's heart, and a vision came to him of a
Christian church in which devotees were burning incense and
lighting candles before Jesus. For three days Sri Ramakrishna
lived under the spell of this experience. On the fourth day,
while he was walking in a grove at Dakshineswar, he saw a
person of serene countenance approaching with his gaze fixed
on him. From the inmost recesses of Sri Ramakrishna's heart
came the realization, 'This is Jesus, who poured out his heart's
blood for the redemption of mankind. This is none other than
Christ, the embodiment of love.' The Son of Man then em-
braced Sri Ramakrishna and entered into him, and Sri Ramakrishna went into samadhi, the state of transcendental consciousness. Thus was Sri Ramakrishna convinced of Christ's
divinity.

Shortly after Sri Ramakrishna's death, nine of his young disciples gathered on a winter night before a sacred fire to take their vows of formal renunciation—henceforth they were to serve God as monks. Their leader, the future Swami Vivekananda, told his brothers the story of Jesus' life, asking them to become Christs themselves, to pledge themselves to aid in the redemption of the world, and to deny themselves as Jesus had done. Later, the monks discovered that this evening had been the Christian Christmas Eve—a very propitious occasion for their vows.

Thus, since the early days of our order, Christ has been honoured and revered by our swamis as one of the greatest of illumined teachers. Many of our monks quote Christ's words to explain and illustrate spiritual truths, perceiving an essential unity between his message and the message of our Hindu seers and sages. Like Krishna and Buddha, Christ did not preach a mere ethical or social gospel but an uncompromisingly spiritual one. He declared that God can be seen, that divine perfection can be achieved. In order that men might attain this supreme goal of existence, he taught the renunciation of worldliness, the contemplation of God, and the purification of the heart through the love of God. These simple and profound truths, stated repeatedly in the Sermon on the Mount, constitute its underlying theme, as I shall try to show in the pages to follow.

July, 1963.   SWAMI PRABHAVANANDA

CHAPTER I

The Beatitudes

MATTHEW 5 : 1-12

BEFORE the time came for Jesus to give his Sermon on the Mount, he travelled all over Galilee preaching. 'And his fame went throughout all Syria,' as St Matthew said. The news spread of an extraordinary teacher, and crowds gathered to see him—as they have done for thousands of years in the Orient and still do at the approach of a God-man. They journeyed 'from Galilee, and from Decapolis, and from Jerusalem, and from Judaea, and from beyond Jordan'. And Jesus taught the multitudes according to their capacity; but his Sermon, which contains his highest teachings, he reserved for his disciples, for the ones who were spiritually ready. He took them to a hillside where they would not be interrupted by those who wanted less than his supreme truth.

And seeing the multitudes, he went up into a mountain: and when he was set, his disciples came unto him:

And he opened his mouth, and taught them, saying, . . .

Every spiritual teacher, whether he is a divine incarnation or an illumined soul, has two sets of teachings—one for the multitude, the other for his disciples. The elephant has two sets of teeth: the tusks with which he defends himself from external difficulties and the teeth with which he eats. The spiritual teacher prepares the way for his message with broad lessons—with his tusks, as it were. The inner truth of religion he reveals only to his intimate disciples. For religion is something which can actually be transmitted. A truly illumined teacher can transmit to us the power which unfolds the divine consciousness latent within us. But the field must be fertile and the soil ready before the seed can be sown.

When crowds came on Sundays to visit Sri Ramakrishna, the most widely revered mystic of modern India, he would speak to them in a general way which benefited them. But when his intimate disciples gathered around him, as I was told by one of them, he would make sure that he was not overheard while giving them the sacred truths of religion. Not that the truths themselves are secret—they are recorded, and anyone can read them. But what he gave to these disciples was more than verbal teachings. In a divine mood he would uplift their consciousness.

Christ taught in the same way. He did not give the Sermon on the Mount to the multitudes, but to his disciples, whose hearts were prepared to receive it. The multitudes are not yet able to understand the truth of God. They do not really want it. My master, Swami Brahmananda, used to say: 'How many are ready? Yes, many people come to us. We have the treasure to give them. But they only want potatoes, onions, and eggplants!'

Any one of us who sincerely wants the treasure, who seeks the truth, can benefit from the message given in the Sermon on the Mount and can become a disciple. Christ, as we shall see in our study of his Sermon, speaks of the conditions of discipleship which we must fulfil—for which we must prepare ourselves. He teaches the ways and means to attain to the purification of our hearts, so that the truth of God may be fully revealed within us.

Blessed are the poor in spirit: for their's is the kingdom of heaven.

In this first beatitude, Christ speaks of the chief characteristic which the disciple must have before he is ready to accept what the illumined teacher has to offer him. He must be poor in spirit; in other words, he must be humble. If a man has

pride in learning, wealth, beauty, or lineage, or has precon-
ceived ideas of what spiritual life is and how he should be
taught, his mind is not receptive to higher teachings. In the
Bhagavad-Gita, the gospel of the Hindus, we read:

'Those illumined souls who have realized the Truth will in-
struct you in the knowledge of Brahman [the transcendent
aspect of God] if you will prostrate yourself before them,
question them, and serve them as a disciple.'

According to an Indian tale, a man came to a teacher and
asked to be made a disciple. The teacher, with his spiritual in-
sight, realized that the man was not ready to be taught. So he
inquired: 'Do you know what you have to do in order to be a
disciple?' The man said he did not, and asked the teacher to
tell him. 'Well,' said the teacher, 'you have to fetch water,
gather fuel, cook, and do many hours of heavy work. You also
have to study. Are you willing to do all that?'

The man said: 'Now I know what the disciple has to do.
Tell me please, what does the teacher do?'

'Oh, the teacher sits and gives spiritual instructions in his
quiet way.'

'Ah, I see!' said the man. 'In that case, I don't want to be a
disciple. Why don't you make me a teacher?'

We all want to be teachers. But before we become teachers
we must learn to be disciples. We must learn to be humble.

Blessed are they that mourn: for they shall be comforted.

As long as we think that we are rich in worldly goods or in
knowledge, we cannot make spiritual progress. When we feel
that we are poor in spirit, when we grieve that we have not
realized the truth of God, then only will we be comforted. No
doubt we all mourn—but for what? For the loss of worldly
pleasures and possessions. But that is not the kind of mourning
of which Christ speaks. The mourning which Christ calls
'blessed' is very rare, because it arises from a sense of spiritual

loss, spiritual loneliness. It is a mourning which necessarily comes before God comforts us. Most of us are quite satisfied with the surface life we are leading. In the back of our minds perhaps we are aware that we lack something, but still we cling to the hope that this lack can be filled by the sense objects of this world.

Sri Ramakrishna used to say: 'People weep rivers of tears because a son is not born or because they cannot get riches. But who sheds even one teardrop because he has not seen God?' This false sense of values is the result of our ignorance. Regarding the nature of this ignorance, the Indian philosopher Shankara said that the subject, the knower (Self or Spirit), is as opposed to the object, the known (non-Self or matter), as light is opposed to darkness. Yet through the influence of maya, the inexplicable power of ignorance, the subject and object have become mixed, so that man habitually identifies the Self with the non-Self. It is very easy to understand intellectually that the true Self is different from the body, just as we are different from the clothes we wear. Yet when the body is diseased, we say: 'I am sick.' Intellectually we can understand that the true Self is different from the mind. Yet when a wave of happiness or suffering arises, we say: 'I am happy,' or 'I am miserable.' Also, we identify ourselves with our relatives and friends: anything happening to them seems to be happening to us. We identify ourselves with our possessions. If we lose our wealth, we feel as if we had lost ourselves. This ignorance is common to all mankind. It can only be removed by the direct knowledge of God. When we begin to feel a spiritual lack within ourselves, when we begin to mourn as Christ wished us to mourn, when we shed even one tear for God, then we prepare the way for the comfort of that divine knowledge.

The kind of mourning that Christ called blessed is expressed in the *Imitation of Christ*:

'O Lord God, when shall I be made one with thee and be molten into thy love, so that I wholly forget myself? Be thou in me, and I in thee; and grant that we may so abide, always together in one.'

We must come to this stage, when we feel that nothing can give us peace except the vision of God. Then God draws man's mind to himself as a magnet draws a needle, and comfort comes.

Blessed are the meek: for they shall inherit the earth.

Ignorance and delusion are characteristic of the unregenerate mind. This ignorance is confirmed and buttressed by our sense of ego—our idea that we are separate from one another and from God. Egotism must be overcome if the mind is to be freed from delusion. Therefore—blessed are the meek. But why does Christ say that they shall inherit the earth? At first sight, this seems difficult to understand. Among the yoga aphorisms of Patanjali (yoga means union with God, also the path to that union) there is one aphorism which corresponds to this beatitude: 'The man who is confirmed in non-stealing becomes the master of all riches.' What is meant by 'non-stealing'? It means that we must give up the egotistic delusion that we can possess things, that anything can belong exclusively to us as individuals. We may think: 'But we are good people. We do not steal anything! Whatever we have, we have worked for and earned. It belongs to us by right.' But the truth is that nothing at all belongs to us. Everything belongs to God. When we regard anything in this universe as ours, we are appropriating God's possession.

What then is meekness? It is to live in self-surrender to God, free from the sense of 'me' and 'mine'. This does not mean that we should get rid of wealth, family, and friends; but we should get rid of the idea that they belong to us. They belong to God. We should think of ourselves as God's servants to whose care he has entrusted his creatures and possessions. As soon as we understand this truth and give up our deluded individual claims, we find that in the truest sense everything belongs to us after all.

Conquerors who try to become masters of the world by force of arms never inherit anything except worry, trouble, and headaches. Misers who accumulate huge wealth are only chained to their gold, they never really possess it. But the man who has given up his sense of attachment experiences the advantages which possessions afford without the misery which possessiveness brings.

Many people dislike this saying of Christ's because they think that the meek can never achieve anything. They think that no happiness is to be had in life unless one is aggressive. When they are told to give up the ego, to be meek, they are afraid that they will lose everything. But they are wrong. In the words of Swami Brahmananda:

'People who live in the senses think that they are enjoying life. What do they know about enjoyment? Only those who are filled with divine bliss really enjoy life.'

But arguments will not prove this truth. You have to experience it; then only will you be convinced.

If a spiritual aspirant sincerely follows Christ's teaching of meekness, he will find it very practical. He will find that anger and resentment can be conquered by gentleness and love. The Chinese mystic Lao Tzu expressed this truth by saying:

'Of the soft and weak things in the world, none is weaker than water. But in overcoming that which is firm and strong, nothing can equal it. That which is soft conquers the hard. Rigidity and hardness are companions of death. Softness and tenderness are companions of life.'

By sincerely giving up the ego to God, by being meek, we will gain everything. We will inherit the earth.

Blessed are they which do hunger and thirst after righteousness: for they shall be filled.

What is the righteousness for which Christ wants us to hunger and thirst? It is the righteousness which in a number of passages in the Old Testament is practically synonymous with salvation—in other words, with deliverance from evil, and union with God. This righteousness therefore is not what we ordinarily think of as moral virtues or good qualities, not relative good as opposed to evil or relative virtue as opposed to vice, but absolute righteousness, absolute goodness. The hunger and thirst after the righteousness of which Christ speaks is a hunger and thirst after God himself.

It has already been pointed out that most of us do not really want God. If we analyse ourselves, we shall find that our interest in God is not nearly as strong as our interest in all kinds of worldly objects. But even a slight desire to know the divine reality is a beginning that can lead us higher. We must start with self-effort. We must struggle to develop love for the Lord by practising recollectedness of him, by prayer, worship, and meditation. As we practise these spiritual disciplines, our slight desire to realize him will become intensified until it is a raging hunger and a burning thirst.

To those who asked him how to realize God, Sri Ramakrishna would say:

'Cry to him with a yearning heart, and then you will see him. After the rosy light of dawn out comes the sun; likewise, longing is followed by the vision of God. He will reveal himself to you if you love him with the combined force of these three attachments: the attachment of a miser to his wealth, that of a mother to her new-born child, and that of a chaste wife to her husband. Intense longing is the surest way to God-vision.'

We must learn to direct all our thoughts and all our energy consciously towards God. One gigantic thought-wave must be raised in the mind, engulfing all the cravings and passions which distract us from the spiritual goal. When the mind thus becomes one-pointed and concentrated upon God, we shall be filled with righteousness.

There is a story of a disciple who asked his teacher, 'Sir, how can I realize God?'

'Come along,' said the teacher, 'I will show you.'

He took the disciple to a lake, and both plunged in. Suddenly the teacher reached over and pressed the disciple's head under water. A few moments later he released him and asked: 'Well, how did you feel?'

'Oh, I was dying for a breath of air!' gasped the disciple.

Then the teacher said: 'When you feel that intensely for God, you won't have to wait long for his vision.'

Blessed are the merciful: for they shall obtain mercy.

One of the yoga aphorisms of Patanjali, the father of Hindu psychology, corresponds to this beatitude:

'Undisturbed calmness of the mind is attained by cultivating friendliness towards the happy, mercy and compassion for the unhappy, delight in the virtuous, and indifference towards the wicked.'

To be merciful is one of the conditions necessary before we can receive the truth of God. Envy, jealousy, hatred—these are some of the universal weaknesses inborn in man. They are linked with our ego-sense which stems from ignorance. How are we to overcome them? By raising an opposite wave of thought. When somebody is happy, we should not be jealous of him; we should try to realize our friendship and unity and be happy with him. When somebody is unhappy, we should not be glad; we should feel sympathy and be merciful. When a man is good, do not be envious. When he is bad, do not hate him. Be indifferent to the wicked. Any thought of hate, even so-called 'righteous hatred' of evil, will raise a wave of hatred and evil in our own minds, increasing our ignorance and restlessness. We cannot think of the Lord or love him until this thought-wave has subsided. If we want to find God, we have to become God-like in mercy.

My master used to say: 'What is the difference between man and God? Man, if you hurt him but once, will forget all your previous kindnesses to him and remember the one time you failed. But if you forget God and sin against him hundreds of times, still he will forgive all your faults and remember the few times that you sincerely prayed to him. Sin exists only in man's eyes; God does not look to man's sins.'

Blessed are the pure in heart: for they shall see God.

In every religion we find two basic principles: the ideal to be realized and the method of realization. Every scripture of the world has proclaimed the truth that God exists and that the purpose of man's life is to know him. Every great spiritual teacher has taught that man must realize God and be reborn in spirit. In the Sermon on the Mount the attainment of this ideal is expressed as perfection in God: 'Be ye therefore perfect, even as your Father which is in heaven is perfect.' And the method of realization which Christ teaches is the purification of the heart which leads to that perfection.

What is this purity which we must have before God reveals himself to us? We all know of people whom we would describe as pure in an ethical sense, but they have not seen God. What is the reason? Ethical life, the steady practice of moral virtues, is needed as a preparation for spiritual life and therefore is a fundamental teaching in every religion. But it does not enable us to see God. It is like the foundation of a house; it is not the superstructure.

What is the test of purity? Try to think of God now, this very moment. What do you find? The thought of his presence passes through your mind, perhaps like a flash. Then many distractions begin. You are thinking of everything else in the universe *but* God. These distractions show that the mind is still impure, and therefore not ready to receive the vision of

God. The impurities consist of various impressions which the mind has gathered from birth to birth. The impressions have been created and stored in the subconscious part of the mind as the result of an individual's thoughts and actions, and in their totality they represent his character. These impressions must be dissolved completely before the mind can be considered pure. St Paul referred to this overhauling of the mind in his Epistle to the Romans, when he said: '. . . be ye transformed by the renewing of your mind.'

According to Yoga Psychology, there are five root causes of impressions in the mind. First is ignorance, in a universal sense, of our divine nature. God dwells in and around us, but we are not conscious of this truth. Instead of seeing God, we see this universe of many names and forms which we believe to be real—just as a man who sees a rope lying on the ground in the dusk may believe it, in the twilight of his ignorance, to be a snake. Secondly, there is the sense of ego, projected by this ignorance, which makes us think of ourselves as separate from God and from one another. Out of the sense of ego we develop attachment and also aversion; we are attracted by one thing, repelled by another. Both desire and hatred are obstacles in the path to God. The fifth cause of impure mental impressions is the thirst to live, which Buddha calls tanha, and to which Christ refers when he says: 'For whosoever will save his life shall lose it.' This clinging to life, or fear of death, is natural to all, good and bad alike. Only the illumined soul has no ignorance, no sense of ego, no attachment, no aversion, and no fear of death; the impressions have all vanished.

Even if God were to offer us spiritual enlightenment this very moment, we would refuse to accept it. Even if we have been seeking God, we momentarily draw back in panic when we are about to have his vision. We instinctively cling to our surface life and consciousness, afraid to give them up, even though doing so means passing into an infinite consciousness, compared to which our normal perceptions are, as the Bhagavad-Gita says, 'like a thick night and a sleep'.

Swami Vivekananda, the apostle of Sri Ramakrishna, was

from his boyhood a pure soul longing for God. Yet he experienced that same fear. When he first came to his future
master, Sri Ramakrishna gave him a touch, and his spiritual
vision began to open. Then Vivekananda cried out: 'What are
you doing to me? I have my parents at home!' And Sri Ramakrishna said: 'Oh, you too!' He saw that even this great soul
was subject to the universal clinging to surface consciousness.

There are many ways to purify the heart. As we shall see,
Christ teaches them throughout his Sermon. The main principle in all the methods is devotion to God. The more we think
of the Lord and take refuge in him, the more we shall love him
—and the purer our hearts will become.

The principle of centring our life in God is equally affirmed
by holy men of the Jewish, the Christian, and the Hindu
traditions. 'The Lord is my strength and my shield,' said the
Psalmist. In the *Imitation of Christ*, we read: 'Thou art my
hope, thou art my trust, thou my comfort. . . . I find all infirm
and unstable whatever I behold outside thee.'

Swami Brahmananda taught his disciples this same truth:
'Hold on to the pillar of God.' In India, the children first hold
on to a pillar, and then spin round it—without danger of falling. In the same way, as long as we hold on to God, we realize
that the experiences of pleasure and pain are impermanent in
their very nature. And as we continue to hold on to the pillar
of God and become devoted to him, our passions and cravings,
which obstruct God-vision, lose their strength.

One method to calm the mind and grow in purity is to try
to feel that we are already pure and divine. This is not a delusion. God created us in his own image; purity and divinity
are therefore basically our nature. If we cry all our lives that
we are sinners, we only weaken ourselves. Sri Ramakrishna
used to say that by repeating constantly, 'I am a sinner', one
really becomes a sinner. One should have such faith as to be
able to say: 'I have chanted the holy name of God. How can
there be any sin in me?'

'Admit your sins to the Lord,' Sri Ramakrishna taught, 'and
vow not to repeat them. Purify body, mind, and tongue by

chanting his name. The more you move towards the light, the
farther you will be from darkness.'

*Blessed are the peacemakers: for they shall be called the
children of God.*

Only when we have been illumined by the unitive knowledge of God do we really become his children and peacemakers. Of course it is true that we are always his children,
even in ignorance. But in ignorance our ego is 'unripe'; it is
self-assertive and forgets God. We cannot bring peace until we
have realized our oneness with God and with all beings. In the
state of transcendental consciousness (that perfect divine union
which the Hindus call samadhi) the illumined soul has no ego;
his ego is merged in the Godhead. When he returns to a lower
plane of consciousness he is again aware of his individuality;
but now he has a 'ripe' sense of ego which does not create any
bondage for himself or for others. In illustration of this ripe ego
the Hindu scriptures speak of a burnt rope; it has the appearance of a rope, but it cannot tie anything. Without such an
ego it would not be possible for a God-man to live in a human
form and teach. When I was a young monk, a disciple of Sri
Ramakrishna once said to me:

'There are times when it becomes impossible for me to teach.
No matter where I look I see only God, wearing so many
masks, playing in so many forms. Who is the teacher then?
Who is to be taught? But when my mind comes down from
that plane, then I see your faults and weaknesses and try to
remove them.'

There is a passage in the Bhagavata, a popular devotional
scripture of the Hindus, which reads: 'He in whose heart God
has become manifest brings peace, and cheer, and delight everywhere he goes.' He is the peacemaker Christ speaks of in the
Beatitudes. I am reminded of a life that I have seen—the life
of my master, Swami Brahmananda. Whoever came into his

presence would feel a spiritual joy. And wherever he went he brought with him an atmosphere of festivity.

In one of our monasteries there were a number of young postulants, not yet trained, fresh from school. When they had been together a short time, their old tendencies began to assert themselves, and the boys formed cliques and quarrelled. A senior swami of our order went to investigate. He questioned everybody and soon discovered the ringleaders. Then he wrote to Swami Brahmananda, who was the head of our order, that these boys were unfitted for monastic life and should be expelled. My master answered: 'Don't do anything about it. I am coming myself.' When he arrived at the monastery, he did not question anyone. He just started living there. He insisted on only one thing—that all the boys should meditate in his presence regularly every day. The boys soon forgot their quarrels. The whole atmosphere of the place became uplifted. By the time Swami Brahmananda left, two or three months later, perfect harmony had been established in the monastery. No one had to be expelled. The minds and hearts of the postulants were transformed.

When I first came to our monastery at Belur, two young boys quarrelled and came to blows. Swami Premananda, the abbot, saw this and asked Brahmananda, his brother disciple, to send the boys away. My master told him: 'Brother, they have not come here as perfect souls. They have come to you to attain perfection. Do something for them!' Swami Premananda said: 'You are right!' He called all of us monastics together and brought us to Swami Brahmananda. With folded hands he asked my master to bless us. Swami Brahmananda raised his hand over our heads, and one by one we prostrated before him. Speaking from my own experience, I can only say that that blessing was like a cooling spring to a fevered body. It gave one an inner exaltation which could be felt but not described. All our troubles were forgotten, and our hearts were full of love. This is how a real peacemaker affects us. When our hearts are uplifted by his presence, we no longer have any desire to quarrel, because we are engaged in the love of God.

*Blessed are they which are persecuted for righteousness'
sake: for their's is the kingdom of heaven.*

*Blessed are ye, when men shall revile you, and persecute
you, and shall say all manner of evil against you falsely, for
my sake.*

*Rejoice, and be exceeding glad: for great is your reward in
heaven: for so persecuted they the prophets which were before
you.*

Worldly people do not understand the value of the spiritual
life. Often they mock at the spiritual aspirant, and sometimes
they revile him and try to do him an injury. But the religious
man does not react to this. His mind is fixed in God; therefore
he feels the unity, he sees the ignorance, and he is merciful.
But whether he is criticized or harmed, he does not compromise; he does not choose to please worldly people.

There is a story of a young monk who was travelling. When
he got tired, he lay down under a tree. Having no pillow, he
got a few bricks and rested his head on them. Some women
were going along the road to fetch water from the river. When
they saw the monk lying there, they said to each other: 'Look
—that young man has become a monk, and yet he can't do
without the idea of a pillow. He has to have bricks instead.'
They went on their way, and the monk said to himself: 'They
were quite right to criticize me.' So he threw the bricks away,
and lay down again with his head on the earth. Presently, the
women returned, and saw that the bricks were gone; and they
exclaimed contemptuously: 'That's a fine sort of monk! He
feels insulted because we said he had a pillow. Now, look—
he has thrown his pillow away!' Then the monk thought: 'If
I have a pillow, people criticize me; and if I don't have a pillow,
that doesn't suit them either. You can't please them; let me try
to please God alone.'

No really spiritual man will perform any action for the sake
of making a good impression upon others, or in order to create
prestige for himself. He sometimes feels just the opposite—that
if he has to go contrary to the whole world for the sake of God

he will do it, and do it alone; he does not care what others think of him.

Normally, when someone speaks ill of us or tries to harm us, we instinctively want to appease our ego rather than please God; and so we feel the urge to retaliate. But if we give in to this urge, we hurt not only someone else but ourselves as well; for when we are angry or resentful, we cut ourselves off from the thought of God. Therefore all the great spiritual teachers have taught, as Christ did, not to retaliate, not to resist evil, but to pray for those who revile and persecute us.

Of course, perfect non-resistance cannot be followed by all. For a man who does not live in a state of God-consciousness, who sees evil, it is a duty to resist evil. For him, non-resistance would not be a virtue but an excuse for hypocrisy or cowardice. Before an individual is ready to turn the other cheek he must be spiritually evolved; he must have attained purity of heart. (This is discussed in greater detail in chapter 3.) Only an illumined soul, one who sees God in all beings, can maintain perfect patience, forbearance, and tranquillity in the midst of the conflicts and contradictions of life.

Throughout the history of religion we find such illumined souls—saints and divine incarnations who lived the ideal of non-resistance and forgiveness. Christ praying on the Cross, 'Father, forgive them; for they know not what they do', is one of the greatest and most famous examples. In our own age, Sri Ramakrishna exemplified the same ideal, as the following incident illustrates.

A priest at the Dakshineswar temple garden, where Sri Ramakrishna was living, became jealous because Mathur Babu, the manager of the temple estate, was fond of Sri Ramakrishna and would go to any trouble to see to his comfort. This priest thought that Sri Ramakrishna had cast a magic spell on Mathur to bring him under his control. Again and again he begged Sri Ramakrishna to reveal to him the secret formula for his success. The Master told him repeatedly that he had used no occult powers, but the priest did not believe him. One day, when Sri Ramakrishna was alone in his room, absorbed in the consciousness of God, the priest entered unobserved and kicked and beat him until he was bleeding. Sri Ramakrishna did not mention the incident to anyone until much later, after the priest had been asked to leave the temple for another reason. When he told Mathur about it, the latter exclaimed: 'Father, why didn't you let me know sooner! I would have chopped off his head!' Sri Ramakrishna replied: 'That's why I didn't tell you. . . . It was not his fault. He sincerely believed that I controlled you by a magic spell. I am to blame, because I could not convince him that I was telling the truth.'

Christ tells us that the reward for those who are persecuted for God's sake is heaven. And so the reward of the illumined soul, who does not react to any injury done to him, is immediate, because he knows that heaven is always present within him as well as without, even in this life. He sees God, as Atman, dwelling within his own heart. He sees God, as Brahman, pervading the whole universe. He worships God in every creature. People may think that the persecuted saint is suffering. They do not realize that his mind, absorbed in God, has transcended the physical consciousness, and that the saint therefore has overcome the tribulations of this world even while living on earth. In the words of the Bhagavad-Gita:

> His mind is dead
> To the touch of the external:
> It is alive
> To the bliss of the Atman.
> Because his heart knows Brahman
> His happiness is for ever.

CHAPTER II

The Salt of the Earth

MATTHEW 5 : 13-37

Ye are the salt of the earth: but if the salt have lost his savour, wherewith shall it be salted? it is thenceforth good for nothing, but to be cast out, and to be trodden under foot of men.

IN India, when a disciple comes to a teacher, the teacher tries first of all to give him a firm faith in himself, and a feeling that weakness and cowardice and failure have no part in his true nature. In the second book of the Bhagavad-Gita, almost the first words which Sri Krishna, the divine incarnation, says to Arjuna are: 'What is this weakness? It is beneath you. . . . Shake off this cowardice!'

Just as you can see the contents of a cupboard through its glass doors, a great teacher can see into your heart. But he does not condemn you for your faults and weaknesses. He knows human nature. Because he realizes that when you feel weak and depressed you cannot achieve anything, cannot grow spiritually, he gives you confidence in yourself.

The teacher sees not merely what you are at present, but also the capacities you will develop. Many years ago a young swami, who was about to leave India to preach in America, went to see Swami Turiyananda. When this great disciple of Sri Ramakrishna praised the young monk highly, the latter protested: 'But sir, I don't have any of the qualities you are praising!' Then Turiyananda said: 'What do you know about yourself? I see what you are going to unfold!' We all have the power to unfold the divinity latent within us, but the teacher gives us confidence in our ability to do it.

At the same time we must remember the beatitude: 'Blessed are the meek . . .' Meekness and faith in oneself must go together. The faith which Christ instilled in his disciples by calling them 'the salt of the earth' was not faith in the lower self, the ego, but faith in the higher Self, faith in God within. With such faith comes self-surrender, freedom from any sense of ego.

Sri Ramakrishna illustrated this truth with an incident from Hindu mythology. He told how Radha, the foremost of the shepherdesses, whom Sri Krishna loved best, became apparently very egotistical. When the other shepherdesses complained to Sri Krishna about her, he suggested that they ask Radha. 'Certainly I have an ego,' said Radha. 'But whose ego is it? It is not mine, for everything I have belongs to Krishna.' A person who has surrendered everything to God has no ego in the ordinary sense. He cannot be vain or proud. He has strong faith in the true Self within him, which is one with God.

This saying of Jesus, 'Ye are the salt of the earth . . .' reminds me of a saying my master used to quote to us:

'You have the grace of God, you have the grace of the guru [the spiritual teacher], and you have the grace of God's devotees; but for the lack of one grace you may be cast out.'

What is that one grace? It is the grace of one's own mind, the will to struggle for perfection. If, in spite of all those graces which would otherwise make us 'the salt of the earth', we lack the grace of our own minds, we may be 'trodden under foot of men'. We must strive hard to surrender ourselves wholeheartedly to God—in order that the divinity within us may become manifest.

Ye are the light of the world. A city that is set on an hill cannot be hid.

Neither do men light a candle, and put it under a bushel,

*but on a candlestick; and it giveth light unto all that are in
the house.*

A great spiritual teacher gathers pure souls around him and
teaches them, not only by word of mouth, but by actual trans-
mission of spirituality. He does not simply give them self-con-
fidence; he actually illumines the hearts of his disciples and
makes them the light of the world. For only those who have
obtained illumination through union with the light which
dwells in the hearts of all can become the light of the world.
Only such illumined ones are fit to teach mankind; only they
can carry on the message of a divine incarnation. When Sri
Ramakrishna met anyone who wished to teach the word of
God, he would ask: 'Have you the divine commission?' Only
he who has seen God can receive his commission, his direct
command to teach. Religion degenerates when taught by un-
illumined men. It is no good relying on a degree at a theological college; books cannot give illumination. One may have
studied scriptures, history, philosophy—one may be versed in
theology, dogmas, and doctrines, and give wonderful sermons
—and yet be a baby when it comes to spiritual life. In order
to transform people's lives, one must first light one's own
candle.

According to Vedanta, there are two kinds of knowledge.
The first, the lower, consists of academic knowledge, such as
science and philosophy. Even knowledge of the scriptures is
considered lower knowledge. The second, the higher knowledge,
is the immediate perception of God. A man who is enlightened
by this higher knowledge does not need encyclopedic informa-
tion in order to expound the scriptures; he teaches from inner
experience.

Swami Adbhutananda, one of Sri Ramakrishna's disciples,
was such an enlightened man. Among his brother monks he
was unique in that he had had no formal education at all. He
came to Sri Ramakrishna as a young servant boy who did not
even know how to sign his name. Sri Ramakrishna tried to
teach him the Bengali alphabet, but Adbhutananda could not

manage to read even the first vowel correctly. And yet we who were privileged to meet him in his later life saw the wisdom of this unlettered man. One day, several young monks came across a difficult passage in the Upanishads, the ancient scriptures of the Hindus. They could not understand it, although they referred to a number of commentaries. Finally they asked Adbhutananda for an explanation. As the Swami did not know Sanskrit, the young monks phrased the passage in his vernacular. Adbhutananda thought for a moment; then he said: 'I've got it!' Using a simple illustration, he explained the passage to them, and they found wonderful meaning in it.

A man who has seen God does not need academic knowledge in order to teach religion. His heart has been purified and illumined, and his light shines forth and gives comfort to everyone. He does not have to go out looking for disciples. Sri Ramakrishna used to say that when the lotus blossoms the bees come from all around, of their own accord, to gather the honey. 'Make that lotus blossom!' he used to tell his disciples.

When such an illumined soul appears, and spiritual aspirants gather around him, they cannot help thinking of God and loving him. In the presence of such a soul they feel that God-realization is easy. This was my own experience at the feet of Sri Ramakrishna's disciples. It is not hard to understand; there is no mystery about it. When you go to visit a lawyer, what kind of thoughts come into your mind? Thoughts about legal matters. With a doctor, you think about sickness and medicine. These thoughts come to you because the person you are with at the moment is living in that particular atmosphere. So, also, with a holy man. You may not know anything about him, but this is the test: When you come into his presence, the thought ot God will come to you—even though the holy man may be talking of something quite different.

Of course, you have to be a seeker after the truth of God in order to be susceptible to a spiritual atmosphere. If you are not interested in God-realization, Christ himself may stand before you to teach you, and you will not appreciate him or recognize his greatness. You will turn from him as the many turned from him two thousand years ago. But if you are a spiritual aspirant and come into the presence of an illumined soul, you cannot do other than glorify God, because in his presence you will feel the presence of the Father. This is what Jesus was speaking of when he said to his disciples:

Let your light so shine before men, that they may see your good works, and glorify your Father which is in heaven.

And then he said:

Think not that I am come to destroy the law, or the prophets: I am not come to destroy, but to fulfil.

For verily I say unto you, Till heaven and earth pass, one jot or one tittle shall in no wise pass from the law, till all be fulfilled.

Whosoever therefore shall break one of these least commandments, and shall teach men so, he shall be called the least in the kingdom of heaven: but whosoever shall do and teach them, the same shall be called great in the kingdom of heaven.

Jesus here speaks of the mission of the divine incarnation, called the avatar by the Hindus and the Son of God by the Christians.

The concept of the avatar evolved from the theory of the Logos in both Western and Eastern philosophy. In the West, the theory of the Logos was first developed by the Greeks to bridge the gulf that separates man from God, the known from the unknown. In its earliest uses the Logos was identified with one or another of the physical elements. Plato projected the Logos as the cosmic purpose, the supreme Good, under which all lesser ideas—i.e., eternal archetypes of things, relations, qualities, and values—are subsumed. Later, the Stoics denied the validity of Plato's supersensual archetypes. They perceived the principle of reason to be immanent and active in the universe. Philo, an Alexandrian Jew and contemporary of Jesus, combined Stoic reason with Plato's transcendentalism,

and added them to Hebraism. He declared that the Logos was
not only immanent in the universe but was transcendent as
well, one with God. The author of the Fourth Gospel then used
Philo's Logos theory as the basis for his interpretation of the
life of Christ, but gave it new vision to serve the theological
needs of Christianity. In addition to attributing a real person-
ality to the Logos, he emphasized, not its creative aspect but its
redemptive function, its communication of spirituality to men.
He stressed, moreover, the conception of the Logos as Word
rather than reason, interpreting it as an expression of the
divine will, an outpouring of God's goodness, power, light, and
love. To quote St John:

'In the beginning was the Word, and the Word was with God,
and the Word was God. . . . And the Word was made flesh,
and dwelt among us, (and we beheld his glory, the glory as of
the only begotten of the Father,) full of grace and truth.'

The Logos, the 'only begotten of the Father', was 'made flesh'
in Jesus Christ.

In the Vedas (most ancient of the world's scriptures) we find
passages which are almost identical with the opening sentence
of the Gospel according to St John: 'In the beginning was the
Lord of Creatures; second to him was the Word.' 'The Word
was verily Brahman.' According to the Hindus, Brahman con-
ditioned by maya, his creative power (which is the basis of
mind and matter), is first manifested as the eternal undifferen-
tiated Word, out of which the concrete sensible world then
evolves. To the Hindus, therefore, the Word is incarnated in
all beings, each of whom may directly realize God through the
divine power of the Word. But like St John, Hindus believe
that in a special sense the Logos is made flesh in the avatar—
the avatar being the descent of God, whereas the ordinary man
ascends towards God.

There is this important difference between the Hindu and
Christian concepts of divine incarnation: Christians believe in
a unique historical event, that God was made flesh once and

for all time in Jesus of Nazareth. Hindus, on the other hand, believe that God descends as man many times, in different ages and forms.

In support of the view that Jesus was God's unique representative on earth, Christians often quote his saying: 'I am the way, the truth, and the life: no man cometh unto the Father, but by me.' But when we study the sayings of other world teachers we find that they made almost identical statements, equally declaring themselves to be incarnations of the Godhead. For example, Sri Krishna says:

'I am the goal of the wise man, and I am the way.' 'I am the end of the path, the witness, the Lord, the sustainer. I am the place of abode, the beginning, the friend and the refuge.' 'Fools pass blindly by the place of my dwelling here in the human form; and of my majesty they know nothing at all, who am the Lord, their soul.' 'Fill your heart and mind with me, adore me, make all your acts an offering to me, bow down to me in self-surrender. If you set your heart upon me thus, and take me for your ideal above all others, you will come into my Being.'

Similarly, Buddha reveals that he is the way: 'You are my children, I am your father; through me you have been released from your sufferings. I myself having reached the other shore, help others to cross the stream; I myself having attained salvation, am a saviour of others; being comforted, I comfort others and lead them to the place of refuge.' 'My thoughts are always in the truth. For lo! my self has become the truth. Whosoever comprehends the truth will see the Blessed One.'

What are we to do? Whose words shall we accept—Jesus' or Krishna's or Buddha's? The point is this: If we take the 'I' or 'me' of these teachers to refer to a mere historical man, we can never understand their statements. We must know that when Jesus, Krishna, and Buddha say 'I' or 'me', they are not asserting the ego, the lower self, as ordinary embodied souls do.

They are asserting their divinity, their identity with the universal Self. They are telling us that the Father, the God-head, is reached through the grace of the Son, the incarnation. To the Hindu, the statements of these avatars are not con-tradictory—they are equally true, evoked by the same divine inspiration. Therefore the Hindu accepts all the great sons of God who are worshipped by different religions.

Of course the validity of the avatars is not proved by their claim to be the way of enlightenment or salvation. First, it is revealed by their unique power to transmit spirituality and transform men's lives by touch, look, or wish. Jesus manifested this power when he breathed on his disciples and said to them, 'Receive ye the Holy Ghost'. Sri Krishna manifested this power when he gave Arjuna divine sight, so that the disciple might see the universal form of God. Secondly, the validity of the avatars is shown by the revelation of their divinity in transfiguration. Jesus appeared transfigured before Peter, James, and John. Sri Krishna appeared transfigured before Arjuna, as described in the eleventh chapter of the Gita. The life and Gospel of Sri Ramakrishna record instances in which the master gave the realization of God to his disciples by touch and appeared transfigured to several devotees in the form of their chosen aspect of God.

But, the question may be asked, why should God have descended as man more than once? What purpose was accom-plished? An answer may be found in the Hindu theory, borne out by history, that spiritual culture moves in waves, a re-peated surging and falling. After a fall in a nation's spiritual life, when truth and righteousness have been neglected and forgotten, an avatar is born to relight the flame of religion in the heart. Sri Krishna says:

> When goodness grows weak,
> When evil increases,
> I make myself a body.
>
> In every age I come back
> To deliver the holy,

To destroy the sin of the sinner,
To establish righteousness.

As if to fulfil Sri Krishna's promise, Buddha appeared. At the time of Buddha's birth, spiritual culture in India was at a low ebb; it consisted wholly in the observance of rituals and sacrifices, for people had forgotten the simple fact that religion is primarily a matter of direct experience. Similarly, at the time of Jesus' advent, the externals of the Jewish faith were usurping its inner truth. He came to purify and revivify the religion of the Jews.

From time to time, then, a divine incarnation is needed to re-establish the eternal spirit of religion. By his living example the incarnation shows mankind how to be perfect even as the Father in heaven is perfect. The avatar thus really becomes the way, the truth, and the life. But it is always the same supreme Spirit which embodies itself in the avatar. God is one without a second. He who came as Sri Krishna, and as Buddha, came again as Christ, and as other avatars; he merely chose a different dress. To suit the particular needs of successive ages, with each coming, God reveals a new and characteristic presentation of the eternal truth of religion.

When an avatar is born on earth, he assumes the human body with certain consequent limitations and sufferings, such as hunger and thirst, illness and death. But his advent differs radically from the birth of ordinary embodied souls. In the words of Jesus: 'Ye are from beneath; I am from above.' According to the Hindu view, ordinary souls are born in consequence of their karmas (the effects of their thoughts and deeds of the past). They are born in a particular environment, with particular aptitudes dictated by the desires and tendencies they have created in a previous life. They are products of evolution; they are tied by the fetters of ignorance and live under the spell of maya, the veiling power of Brahman, which makes the absolute reality appear as the universe of many names and forms. They are slaves of prakriti, of primordial nature.

The birth of a Krishna, a Buddha, or a Jesus, however, is the result of free choice. He has no karmas, no cravings or past tendencies. He does not yield to the domination of maya but puts maya under subjection. He appears in human form solely for the purpose of doing good, out of compassion for mankind. Sri Krishna says:

> I am the birthless, the deathless,
> Lord of all that breathes.
> I seem to be born:
> It is only seeming,
> Only my maya.
> I am still master
> Of my prakriti,
> The power that makes me.
>
> He who knows the nature
> Of my task and my holy birth
> Is not reborn
> When he leaves this body:
> He comes to me.

Compare with these last lines the words of the Bible: 'But as many as received him, to them gave he power to become the sons of God, even to them that believe on his name.'

To worship a Christ or a Krishna is to worship God. It is not, however, to worship a man as God, not to worship a person. It is to worship God himself, the impersonal-personal Existence, in and through the incarnation; it is to adore him as one with the eternal Spirit, transcendent as the Father and immanent in all hearts. In this context, St Paul's testimony about Christ is of special relevance. He says:

'For in him dwelleth all the fulness of the Godhead bodily. And ye are complete in him, which is the head of all principality and power.'

Of equal weight is St John's statement that the same word which was 'in the beginning' and 'was God' was made flesh in

Christ. In this passage, the author of the Fourth Gospel reminds us that his master was not a mere historical man, but that he is the eternal Christ, one with God from beginningless time. And this view seems to be validated by Jesus, who said: 'Before Abraham was, I am.'

A Hindu, then, would find it easy to accept Christ as a divine incarnation and to worship him unreservedly, exactly as he worships Sri Krishna or another avatar of his choice. But he cannot accept Christ as the *only* Son of God. Those who insist on regarding the life and teachings of Jesus as unique are bound to have great difficulty in understanding them. Any avatar can be far better understood in the light of other great lives and teachings. No divine incarnation ever came to refute the religion taught by another, but to fulfil all religions; because the truth of God is an eternal truth. St Augustine said:

'That which is called the Christian religion existed among the ancients, and never did not exist from the beginning of the human race until Christ came in the flesh, at which time the true religion, which already existed, began to be called Christianity.'

If, in the history of the world, Jesus had been the sole originator of the truth of God, it would be no truth; for truth cannot be originated; it exists. But if Jesus simply unfolded and interpreted that truth, then we may look to others who did so before him, and will do so after him. And, in fact, as we read the teachings of Jesus, we find that he wishes all of us to unfold that truth: 'And ye shall know the truth, and the truth shall make you free.' He has come, he declares, not to destroy the eternally existing truth, but to fulfil. This he did by restating it, giving it new life by presenting it in a new way.

Again and again men forget that these presentations of the divine incarnations are meant to be unfolded in their own lives. They cling too devotedly to the letter, the outward form, of the avatar's message and lose sight of its undying spirit. These are the scribes and pharisees; the jealous guardians of a tradition which has become obsolete. That is why Christ says:

> For I say unto you, That except your righteousness shall
> exceed the righteousness of the scribes and Pharisees, ye shall
> in no case enter into the kingdom of heaven.

The scribes and pharisees forget the first commandment, to
'love the Lord thy God with all thy heart, and with all thy
soul, and with all thy mind'. They are very ethical, upright
men in their own way; but they cling to forms and outward
observances, and this leads them towards intolerance, narrow-
ness, and dogmatism. The righteousness which exceeds the
righteousness of the scribes and pharisees is the very opposite
of this. It is an ethic which regards the observance of forms
and rituals, not as an end in itself, but as a means to enter
into the kingdom of heaven.

God is beyond relative good and evil. He is the absolute
Good. When we unite ourselves with him in our consciousness,
we transcend relative righteousness. This truth has often been
misunderstood. It does not mean that we should condone im-
morality, for ethical life is the very foundation of spirituality.
At the beginning of spiritual life we must consciously abstain
from harming others, from falsehood, theft, incontinence, and
greed; we must observe mental and physical purity, content-
ment, self-control, and recollectedness of God.

But the urge to live a truly ethical life and to practise
spiritual disciplines comes to us only if we try to live the first
commandment—if we learn to love God, and struggle to
realize him. Without that ideal, morality degenerates into the
external decorum of the scribes and pharisees. But when the
first commandment is observed, then the second commandment follows as a matter of course. When we love God, we
must love our neighbour as our self—because our neighbour
is our very Self.

Through the practice of self-control, the inner restraint of
the passions, we develop spiritually towards union with the
absolute Good. The man who attains this ultimate state does

not have to discriminate consciously between right and wrong, or practise self-mastery. Holiness and purity become his very nature. He transcends relative righteousness and enters the kingdom of heaven.

Ye have heard that it was said by them of old time, Thou shalt not kill; and whosoever shall kill shall be in danger of the judgment:

But I say unto you, That whosoever is angry with his brother without a cause shall be in danger of the judgment: and whosoever shall say to his brother, Raca, shall be in danger of the council: but whosoever shall say, Thou fool, shall be in danger of hell fire.

It is not enough to obey the commandment: 'Thou shalt not kill.' Even the thought of killing, of hatred, is as deadly as the act. We may pretend to ourselves that it does not matter what we think, as long as we act rightly. But when the test comes, we always betray ourselves, for the thought controls the act. When the test comes, if our minds are full of hatred, that hatred will express itself in acts of violence and destruction and murder. Standing up in the pulpit and talking about love will not help us; it will not stop war and cruelty, when there is no love in our hearts. Love will not come to us simply because we say we have it, or try to impress other people with the seeming sweetness of our natures. It comes only when we have controlled our passions inwardly and have subdued our ego. Then divine love grows in us, and with it love of our fellow men. But the love of God has to be won through self-discipline, which we have neglected to practise. We have forgotten the aim of life—to realize and see God. That is our whole difficulty, and that is why when Jesus asks us to love our enemies, we are unable to obey him, even if we wish to do so. We do not know how.

We cannot love God and hate our neighbour. If we really love God, we will find him in everyone; so how can we hate another? If we harm anyone, we harm ourselves; if we help

anyone, we help ourselves. All feelings of separateness, ex-
clusiveness and hatred are not only morally wrong, they are
ignorant, because they deny the existence of the omnipresent
Godhead.

*Therefore if thou bring thy gift to the altar, and there re-
memberest that thy brother hath ought against thee;*

*Leave there thy gift before the altar, and go thy way; first
be reconciled to thy brother, and then come and offer thy gift.*

*Agree with thine adversary quickly, whiles thou art in the
way with him; lest at any time the adversary deliver thee to
the judge, and the judge deliver thee to the officer, and thou
be cast into prison.*

*Verily I say unto thee, Thou shalt by no means come out
thence, till thou hast paid the uttermost farthing.*

Until we actually reach oneness with God, it is of course
quite natural that we should have misunderstandings and
quarrels with one another. But we must not let our resentments stay with us, or they will eat into our hearts like cancer.
Christ, who like all truly spiritual teachers was a great psy-
chologist, taught that we must be reconciled as soon as possible
with our brother, even before we offer our gift to God. Anyone
who has practised meditation will immediately understand
how sound this teaching is.

Suppose someone has wronged you, and you feel irritated.
When you begin to meditate, what happens? Prayer and
meditation concentrate the mind and intensify the emotions.
Consequently, the molehill of irritation becomes a mountain of
anger. You start to imagine terrible things about the person
who has wronged you. You find yourself unfit to pray and
meditate, unable to come to God, until you are sincerely reconciled with your brother. There is only one way to feel sincerely
reconciled, and that is to try to see God in all beings, and to
love him in all. If you have been angry with your brother, pray
for him as you pray for yourself—pray that both of you may
grow in understanding and devotion to God. At once, you will

gain spiritually. But if you keep your anger in your heart, you will hurt yourself as well as your brother.

It is taught in Buddhism and in Vedanta that it is a man's duty to pray for others before he prays for himself. He is asked to send a thought of good will towards all beings before he offers himself to God. Such a practice is a significant step towards the attainment of love for our neighbour and for God.

'Agree with thine adversary quickly, whiles thou art in the way with him . . .' Christ is teaching us that we must not waste our time and energy on quarrels and resentment but should re-establish ourselves as quickly as possible in the thought of God. To realize God is our purpose in life; therefore we should try to maintain ourselves in his consciousness with as few and as short interruptions as possible. 'Give up all vain talk,' the Upanishads tell us. 'Know the Atman alone.'

The desire to argue and quarrel is a sign of ego. If you want to find God, you must suppress the ego and humble yourself— not before your adversary, but before God within him. Never submit to a powerful adversary because you fear the consequences of disagreement; that would be cowardice. But discriminate between principles and opinions. There is a Hindi saying: 'Say "yea, yea" to everyone, but keep your own seat firm.' Do not compromise on ideals and principles. But when it comes to opinions, appreciate views differing from yours, and accept them when they merit it. Swami Turiyananda used to say :

'Stubbornness is not strength. Stubbornness merely hides one's weakness. Strong is he who is flexible like steel and does not break. Strong is he who can live in harmony with many people and heed opinions other than his own.'

If you are intolerant of the opinions of others and stubbornly insist on having your own way, you will suffer the consequences until you have 'paid the uttermost farthing'.

Ye have heard that it was said by them of old time, Thou shalt not commit adultery:

But I say unto you, That whosoever looketh on a woman to lust after her hath committed adultery with her already in his heart.

And if thy right eye offend thee, pluck it out, and cast it from thee: for it is profitable for thee that one of thy members should perish, and not that thy whole body should be cast into hell.

And if thy right hand offend thee, cut it off and cast it from thee: for it is profitable for thee that one of thy members should perish, and not that thy whole body should be cast into hell.

It hath been said, Whosoever shall put away his wife, let him give her a writing of divorcement:

But I say unto you, That whosoever shall put away his wife, saving for the cause of fornication, causeth her to commit adultery: and whosoever shall marry her that is divorced committeth adultery.

Here Jesus is speaking of the necessity for self-mastery, for mental control of the passions, particularly lust. Merely refraining from lustful actions is not enough; lustful thoughts must be checked, too.

There are, of course, many teachers who would say: 'Yes, indeed, we agree, an inner check on the passions is certainly necessary. Our young people must use self-control.' But very few of those teachers could answer *why* self-control is needed. That is why young people today question them, and even begin to suspect that the teachers hate pleasure for its own sake because they are too old to take part in it themselves. 'What does it matter what we do,' say the young, 'as long as we don't harm anyone else?' They are perfectly honest and sincere about this.

It is no use telling them that their pleasures are wicked, or that it is wrong to be happy, because they will never believe you: their instincts tell them that you are lying. When you talk about sin, they will disregard you. But if you stop telling them that they are sinful, and begin to tell them that God is inside each one of them; if you hold up the ideal of God-realization, and show them that the struggle for self-discipline is hard but exciting, like training for athletics; if you show them that by dissipating themselves they are cutting themselves off from the greatest joy in life, a joy far greater than all their worldly pleasures—then you will be talking a language they can understand. They may be sceptical, but some of them, at least, will want to try spiritual life for themselves.

The ideal of continence has been so misrepresented in this country that nearly everybody thinks of it as something negative, as a 'don't'. Don't be incontinent, the churches tell us; it is a sin. In this way, for the great majority of people, who instinctively hate 'donts', the idea of continence has become unattractive, and associated with repression, gloom, and cowardice; while the idea of incontinence becomes more and more attractive, and is associated with freedom, fun, and courage. This terrible and destructive misunderstanding, if not corrected, will eventually poison the whole national life. Unless boys and girls can be taught the vital connection between continence and spiritual life, they will gradually waste their powers, they will lose the possibility of spiritual growth and with it all real creativeness, all real awareness.

Continence is not repression; it stores up energy and applies that energy to better uses. It is not an end in itself, but an indispensable means of freeing the mind from distracting passions and keeping it in the consciousness of God. Sex energy controlled becomes spiritual energy. To one who is continent, spiritual growth comes quickly and easily.

Many people think that by being continent they will lose the greatest pleasure the world has to offer: but the strange fact is that they will not really lose anything. As the sex energy is conserved and as it becomes transformed, they will find a new and much more intense pleasure growing inside themselves; and that is the joy of coming closer and closer to union with God.

In the Bhagavad-Gita, the state of mind of the self-controlled man is described as follows:

> Water flows continually into the ocean
> But the ocean is never disturbed:
> Desire flows into the mind of the seer
> But he is never disturbed.
> The seer knows peace:
> The man who stirs up his own lusts
> Can never know peace.
> He knows peace who has forgotten desire.
> He lives without craving:
> Free from ego, free from pride.

The worldly person may think that the peace of the seer is like the peace of the grave. On the contrary, it is an experience of supreme and abiding joy, compared to which the short-lived satisfactions known in the sense life appear insipid and worthless. If we wish to find lasting peace and happiness, we must turn to God. The more we devote ourselves to him, the more the desire for sense gratification will leave us; and chastity and other virtues will naturally unfold in our lives.

Complete lifelong continence is for those who have a special dedication to God, as did Christ's disciples. They were monks, and their master was training them to become teachers of men. Therefore he used emphatic words to remind them that they must preserve continence in thought, word, and deed. They must root out every obstacle in their path, every craving in their minds, and renounce every object of temptation. But because Christ knew that his teaching of total renunciation could not be followed universally, he said (Matthew 19:11-12):

'All men cannot receive this saying, save they to whom it is given. For there are some eunuchs, which were so born from their mother's womb: and there are some eunuchs, which were made eunuchs of men: and there be eunuchs, which have made themselves eunuchs for the kingdom of heaven's sake. He that is able to receive it, let him receive it.'

Lust is in the mind and must be overcome by controlling the mind, but not in a negative way. Thinking lustful thoughts while outwardly observing continence is not self-control. It is nothing but repression. Nor will whipping oneself purify the mind; it only weakens the body. True self-mastery, or inner control, is gained only if men make themselves eunuchs 'for the kingdom of heaven's sake'; if they practise continence because they know worldly pleasures to be tasteless and empty compared to the joy of God.

Again, ye have heard that it hath been said by them of old time, Thou shalt not forswear thyself, but shalt perform unto the Lord thine oaths:

But I say unto you, Swear not at all; neither by heaven; for it is God's throne:

Nor by the earth; for it is his footstool: neither by Jerusalem; for it is the city of the great King.

Neither shalt thou swear by thy head, because thou canst not make one hair white or black.

But let your communication be, Yea, yea; Nay, nay: for whatsoever is more than these cometh of evil.

Sri Ramakrishna used to say that God laughs on two occasions. He laughs when two brothers divide land between them, asserting, 'This side belongs to me, and that side to you'. God laughs, thinking to himself, 'This whole universe is mine; and they say about one little lump of earth, "This side belongs to me, and that side to you!"' God laughs again when the doctor says to the mother weeping because of her child's severe illness, 'Don't worry. I shall cure your child'. The doctor does not realize that no one can save the child if God wills that it should die.

Christ here is telling us the same thing. Although man cannot make 'one hair white or black', in his ignorance he thinks himself the doer. He asserts his ego, forgetting that the power he is using in every thought and every action is the power of God, and that it is God's heaven, God's throne, God's earth that he is trying to usurp. Christ therefore tells us, 'Swear not at all', for when we swear we assert the ego.

Truly spiritual people never plan, 'I will do this, I will do that'. Having surrendered the ego to God, their first thought is, 'If the Lord wills . . .' Their humility stems from the realization that God and his power are working through us—that God is the doer and we are his instruments. This is an actual experience in the lives of saints. A holy man once told me that he lived for some time in a state of consciousness in which he vividly felt that each step he took was guided by the power of God.

'Not I, not I, but thou, O Lord!' The more we become established in this idea, the more we renounce the thought of self, the greater will be our attainment of peace.

CHAPTER III

Resist Not Evil

MATTHEW 5:38-47

Ye have heard that it hath been said, An eye for an eye, and a tooth for a tooth:

But I say unto you, That ye resist not evil: but whosoever shall smite thee on thy right cheek, turn to him the other also.

And if any man will sue thee at the law, and take away thy coat, let him have thy cloke also.

And whosoever shall compel thee to go a mile, go with him twain.

Give to him that asketh thee, and from him that would borrow of thee turn not thou away.

Ye have heard that it hath been said, Thou shalt love thy neighbour, and hate thine enemy.

But I say unto you, Love your enemies, bless them that curse you, do good to them that hate you, and pray for them which despitefully use you and persecute you;

That ye may be the children of your Father which is in heaven: for he maketh his sun to rise on the evil and on the good, and sendeth rain on the just and on the unjust.

For if ye love them which love you, what reward have ye? do not even the publicans the same?

And if ye salute your brethren only, what do ye more than others? do not even the publicans so?

THE highest truth which has been taught by the great spiritual teachers of mankind is that we should love our enemies and not resist evil. Buddha, for instance, said:

'If a villainous bandit were to carve you limb from limb with a two-handled saw, even then the man that should give way to anger would not be obeying my teaching. Even then, be it your task to preserve your hearts unmoved, never to allow an ill word to pass your lips, but always to abide in compassion and good-will, with no hate in your hearts, enfolding in radiant thoughts of love the bandit (who tortures you), and proceeding thence to enfold the whole world in your radiant thoughts of love—thoughts great and beyond measure, in which there is no hatred or trace of harm.'

But although non-resistance has been preached in every great religion, it is a practice which most people find nearly impossible to understand and to follow. It is significant that Jesus, after teaching non-resistance, goes on to say: 'Be ye therefore perfect . . .' In other words, to follow this truth in our own lives would lead us to perfection. And indeed, only he who is perfect, who has realized his union with God, who is able to see the divine Existence in all beings, can turn the other cheek and live in universal love. For a man who has reached perfection, non-resistance is a spontaneous outpouring of his experience of God. Where is evil then? Who is an enemy then?

We know instances of holy men who practised non-resistance in our own age. Once my master, Swami Brahmananda, was practising austere spiritual disciplines in Brindavan, a town associated with Sri Krishna's childhood. While he was sitting alone, in meditation, a stranger came and laid a warm, new blanket beside him. A few minutes later, another stranger came by and took the blanket away. Swami Brahmananda never moved. He smiled to himself, watching the divine play.

Pavhari Baba, a saint of nineteenth-century India, one day surprised a thief in the act of stealing from his ashrama. The thief became frightened and ran away, dropping his bundle of stolen goods. The holy man took up the bundle, ran after the thief, laid the bundle at his feet, and with folded hands asked him to accept the goods. Free from any sense of ego or possession, Pavhari Baba felt that everything belonged to God; and he actually saw God in all beings, even in the thief. The thief, incidentally, later became Pavhari Baba's disciple.

Perfect non-resistance is rare because few people struggle to achieve the lofty spiritual state which would enable them to practise it. There is a great variety in character and in levels of spiritual growth among mankind. Even if all men were afforded equal opportunities—which all too often they are not —they cannot grow and succeed in the same way and to the same extent, because their temperaments and tendencies differ. Variety and unity in variety make up the uniform law of creation. Take away variety, and the world would end. The facts of birth and death, and of life itself, contradict any theory of equality and uniformity. All men deserve equal opportunities, no doubt. But when it comes to questions of good and evil, the differences between men must be taken into account: they must face situations differently.

These differences pose serious problems in human conduct. In his article, 'The Religious Ground of Humanitarianism', Paul Elmer More tried to solve these problems by making a distinction between worldly and spiritual virtues. He said:

'To apply the laws of the spirit to the activities of this earth is at once a desecration and denial of religion, and a bewildering and unsettling of the social order.'

He declared, in effect, that as we meet those who are not inspired by religious virtues, we cannot, in our relations with them, practise virtues like humility and non-resistance in their highest form; for if we did, the very structure of society would be undermined. In place of these, he would have us practise the Aristotelian or cardinal virtues of justice, temperance, prudence, and fortitude.

Vedanta goes even further than Dr. More in recognizing ethical and behavioural differences. It is a fundamental belief in Vedanta that one Reality, or God, dwells in the hearts of all beings. But God is not manifest equally in all beings, and all beings are not equally living in God. Vedanta consequently accepts the fact that human society has gradations. The implications of this fact were stated by Swami Vivekananda:

'Two ways are left open to us—the way of the ignorant, who think that there is only one way to truth and that all the rest are wrong—and the way of the wise, who admit that, according to our mental constitution or the plane of existence in which we are, duty and morality may vary. The important thing is to know that there are gradations of duty and morality, that the duty of one state of life, in one set of circumstances, will not and cannot be that of another.'

Thus, instead of drawing a sharp line of distinction between worldly and spiritual virtues, as More did, Vedanta indicates the existence of graded virtues—virtues which differ according to the different types and conditions of humanity. This does not mean, however, that the universal ideal of non-resistance and non-violence should be adapted to the individual temperament; for the high spiritual goal of life must be kept in view by all men. But at the same time, different levels of being must be recognized so that everyone may be enabled, step by step, sooner or later, to attain to the supreme Good.

Non-resistance is therefore recognized by Vedanta as the highest virtue, but all people under all circumstances are not expected to live up to it in its highest form. On the contrary, Vedanta points out that for some it is necessary to learn to resist evil and by this means grow in moral strength to a point where they can endure it. Consider the man who does not resist because he is weak or lazy, and will not make the effort to do so. Is there any merit in such non-resistance? Then consider another who knows that he can strike an irresistible blow if he likes, and yet does not strike, but blesses, his enemy. In the words of Vivekananda:

'The one who from weakness does not resist, commits a sin, and therefore cannot receive any benefit from his non-resistance; while the other would commit a sin by offering resistance.'

That is to say, we must gather the power to resist; having gained it, we must renounce it. Then only will non-resistance be a virtue. But if we are weak and lazy, and pretend to ourselves that we are actuated by the highest motives, we do not merit praise. Of the non-resistance which derives from strength, Swami Vivekananda said:

'. . . this non-resistance is the highest manifestation of power in actual possession, and what is called the resisting of evil is but a step on the way towards it.'

Once a young disciple of Sri Ramakrishna was crossing the Ganges in a ferryboat from Calcutta on his way to visit his master. The other passengers in the boat were speaking against Sri Ramakrishna, saying that he was not a man of renunciation but a hypocrite who enjoyed the comforts of life. When the disciple heard this he protested, but the passengers ignored him and continued to criticize Sri Ramakrishna. Then the disciple became very angry. He jumped to his feet and threatened to sink the boat. The passengers saw that he was an athletic youth, well able to carry out his threat. They were frightened and begged his pardon. Not another word was said against Sri Ramakrishna during the rest of the trip. Later, when the disciple reported the incident to Sri Ramakrishna, the Master was displeased. 'Be indifferent to what mean-minded people say,' he told the young man. 'Think what a great crime you were about to commit under the influence of anger!' And he taught him never to offer violence under any circumstances.

However, on a different occasion, another of Sri Ramakrishna's disciples was crossing the Ganges by boat, and once again the passengers were talking against Sri Ramakrishna. The disciple felt distressed but, being of a mild nature, he decided that the passengers were not to be blamed; they were speaking in ignorance because they did not know his master

personally. The disciple felt that he could do nothing about
this, so he kept quiet. Later, when he told Sri Ramakrishna
about the incident, he thought his master would laugh about
it. But Sri Ramakrishna reproved him severely: 'What!' he exclaimed. 'You call yourself my disciple, and you let people
slander me in your presence?'

Sri Ramakrishna's advice seems altogether contradictory, but
the reason for it, of course, is that he was dealing with two
very different individuals. He wished to correct the over-
aggressiveness of the one who was ready to be taught non-
violence and to correct the timidity of the other by teaching
him first to 'resist evil'.

When we realize that duties and conduct must vary to suit
individual lives and circumstances, we can see why Sri Krishna
in the Gita urges Arjuna to fight (a point which has often been
misunderstood), whereas Christ in his Sermon urges his disciples to practise non-resistance. In the Sermon on the Mount,
Christ gives the highest teachings about non-resistance because
he is addressing disciples who are dedicated monks; and he is
speaking to them in surroundings of peace and solitude. The
message of the Gita, however, is given by Sri Krishna on a
battlefield to a householder-disciple, a warrior by profession.
Arjuna has not yet reached the spiritual enlightenment which
would permit him to renounce action. To fight is his duty,
dictated by his character which his past thoughts and actions
have imposed upon him. Therefore Sri Krishna points out to
his disciple: 'Your own nature will drive you to the act.' The
teacher realizes that what Arjuna considers his revulsion from
the act of killing does not stem from spiritual realization but
from cowardice. Not by shirking his duty, but by performing
it and by practising devotion and self-surrender to God, Arjuna
can ultimately transcend the law of cause and effect and realize
the highest spiritual truth.

It is true that from the standpoint of transcendence there is
no duty, no action, no physical universe of name and form—
only Brahman, the Absolute, exists. But before we are united
with Brahman in our consciousness, we must employ a set of

relative values. That is why Sri Krishna teaches Arjuna, and every spiritual aspirant, the way of action from inertia to illumination. We must proceed from where we stand if we are to have true spiritual growth.

But the problem remains: How are we to apply the teaching of non-resistance to our own lives? A householder-devotee of Sri Ramakrishna one day asked the Master what he should do if a wicked person were about to harm him, and in reply Sri Ramakrishna told the following parable.

There was once a holy man who came to a village. The villagers warned him that he must not go along a certain path because a venomous snake, which had killed many people, always lay there. 'It won't hurt me,' said the holy man, and continued on his way. Sure enough, the snake approached, reared its head, hissing and ready to strike; but when it saw the holy man it prostrated humbly at his feet. The sage taught it to give up the idea of biting and killing. According to instructions, the snake, having received initiation into spiritual life with a sacred name of God, crawled off to its hole to pray and meditate; and the holy man proceeded on his way. Soon the boys of the village discovered the change in the character of the snake. Knowing that it was now harmless, they would attack it with sticks and stones whenever it came out of its hole—but the snake would never strike back. After a while, the snake grew so weak from its injuries that it could scarcely crawl. Only rarely, at night, it would come out of its hole in search of food.

When next the holy man came to that village, he was told that the snake was dead. 'That's impossible,' said the sage. 'It cannot die until it has attained the fruit of the holy word with which it was initiated.' He went to the snake's hole and called it. Hearing its teacher's voice, the snake came squirming out, crippled from the blows it had received and terribly thin because it was not getting enough to eat. The holy man questioned it about the reason for its condition. 'Revered sir,' the snake replied, 'you asked me not to harm any creature. I have been living on leaves and fruit. Perhaps that's why I am so thin.' The snake had developed the virtue of forgiveness and had forgotten that the boys had almost killed it. The sage said: 'No, there must be a reason other than want of food that is responsible for your condition. Try to remember.' Then the snake recalled: 'Oh yes, some village boys beat me, but I wouldn't bite them. I just lay silently and suffered their torments.' The snake expected to be praised for not resisting evil. To its great surprise, however, the holy man became quite cross: 'How foolish you are!' he cried. 'I told you not to bite. Did I tell you not to hiss?'

The householder, who must live in society and fulfil his duty towards his family, may need to hiss now and then in order to defend himself against hostile actions. The goody-goody man, who lets himself be cheated and tricked, is foolish, not saintly. But although the householder may protect himself, he must never be malicious or revengeful. He may hiss, but he must never inject venom. The monk, on the other hand, must strive to practise non-violence in its higher form.

The devotee of God who perseveres in his spiritual practices eventually reaches a state in which non-violence in thought, word, and deed is natural to him. Then, with mind absorbed in God and heart purified by devotion, he does spontaneously what Christ asks of him—he loves his enemies, blesses those that curse him, does good to those that hate him, and prays for those who persecute him. Then truly he is the child of his Father in heaven.

CHAPTER IV

Be Ye Therefore Perfect

MATTHEW 5:48-6:8

Be ye therefore perfect, even as your Father which is in heaven is perfect.

IN this sentence Jesus gives the central theme of the Sermon on the Mount. The whole purpose of man's life is stated here. And the same theme is at the heart of every religion: Seek perfection! Realize God!

We have an idea of what perfection might be when it comes to physical objects or intellectual or moral goals, though individual standards may differ. But what is meant by divine perfection? As long as our minds dwell within the world of relativity—within time, space, and causation—we cannot know what this perfection is, because it is absolute. We have only a vague idea that it refers to a state of completion, of abiding peace and fulfilment. Every human being wishes to find fulfilment and perfection—in his relations with other human beings, in his work, in every field of life. But when he achieves the goals the world has to offer, he is still not satisfied. He may be surrounded by a fine family and loyal friends, enjoy wealth and good health, beauty and fame, and nevertheless be haunted by a sense of lack and frustration.

Of course it is quite true that our desires can be temporarily appeased in this world. We can have some measure of pleasure and success. But we always forget that these are impermanent. If we accept pleasure and success, we must be ready to accept pain and failure.

Kapila, a philosopher of ancient India, expressed the state of

perfection negatively as 'complete cessation of misery'. The
Vedic sages tried to express it positively, as Sat, immortal life;
Chit, infinite knowledge; and Ananda, eternal love and bliss.
Behind every human effort there is the desire (unconscious
and misdirected though it may be) to find Sat-chit-ananda—in
other words, the supreme reality, God. But since most of us are
not aware that to find God is our real purpose in life, we continue to repeat the same enjoyments and sufferings over and
over again. We waste our energies in ephemeral achievements,
looking for infinite reward in the finite. Only after we have
passed through many experiences of pleasure and pain does
spiritual discrimination dawn in us. Then we begin to see that
nothing in this world can give us lasting satisfaction. Then we
understand that the desire for abiding happiness, for perfection, can be fulfilled only in the eternal truth of God.

We have the right to aspire to that perfection, for it is our
divine heritage. In the words of St Paul:

'The Spirit itself beareth witness with our spirit, that we are
the children of God: And if children, then heirs; heirs of God
and joint-heirs with Christ . . .'

But where do we find perfection? Where is God? According
to Vedanta, there is a divine Ground, Brahman, underlying the
universe of name and form. It is omnipresent; therefore it
exists within every creature and object in the universe, as well
as beyond them. Considered in its immanent aspect, Brahman
is called the Atman, the Self within, but this is merely a con-
venient term which does not imply any difference between the
two—Atman and Brahman are one. When the mind has been
purified through spiritual disciplines and is able to turn inward
upon itself, man realizes that his true being is Atman-Brah-
man. To uncover this true being, or divinity, which lies hidden
within oneself, is to become perfect. This is the technique of
all mystical practice.

Christ himself taught us to seek God within. In the Gospel
according to St Luke we read: 'The kingdom of God cometh

not with observation: Neither shall they say, Lo here! or, lo there! for, behold, the kingdom of God is within you.' This statement has sometimes been interpreted to mean that Christ lived amidst his disciples on earth. But if we do not accept Christ's statement as referring to the divinity within man, how can we understand his prayer to the Father: 'I in them, and thou in me, that they may be made perfect in one . . .?' Or the Apostle Paul's reminder to the Corinthians: 'Know ye not that ye are the temple of God, and that the Spirit of God dwelleth in you?'

What prevents us from realizing this truth that God is always present within us? It is our ignorance—the false identification of our true nature, which is Spirit, with body, mind, senses, and intellect. 'And the light shineth in darkness; and the darkness comprehended it not.' The light of God is shining, but the veil of our ignorance covers that light. This ignorance is a direct and immediate experience. It can only be removed by another direct and immediate experience—God-realization. The difference between ignorance and God-realization is, as Buddha stated, like that between sleep and awakening.

In our ignorance it is hard for us to believe that God can be realized. In fact, many individuals resist the idea. Yet in every age there have been great souls who saw God, talked with him, and experienced union with him. Teachers like Jesus, Buddha, and Sri Ramakrishna not only realized God but insisted that everyone must do so. A Vedic seer declared: 'I have known that Great Being of effulgent light, beyond all darkness. You also, having known that Truth, go beyond death.' And Jesus declared: 'And ye shall know the truth, and the truth shall make you free.' The experience of that truth is made possible through transformation or, in the words of Jesus, spiritual rebirth: 'Except a man be born again, he cannot see the kingdom of God.' Commenting on this statement, the German mystic Angelus Silesius said: 'Christ may be born a thousand times in Bethlehem, but if he be not born anew within your own heart, you remain eternally forlorn.'

What does it mean to have Christ born anew in our hearts? Ordinarily, the Upanishads tell us, man lives within three states of consciousness: waking, dreaming, and dreamless sleep. In these three states it is not possible to see God. But beyond these three there is a state, called the Fourth, which is known to the mystics—a state which transcends time, space, and causation. It is Christ's kingdom of God. What is experienced in this Fourth is not contradicted at any time by any other experience—unlike fantasies in the dream state, which are contradicted when we wake up. Although the Fourth transcends the senses and the mind, it does not contradict reason. When it illumines the heart, a permanent transformation of character takes place. We are reborn in spirit and become perfect. In this transcendental state, all awareness of the world and of multiplicity is obliterated. Brahman alone exists, and the peace which passeth all understanding is known. The Hindus call this state samadhi; Buddhists call it nirvana; and Christians call it the mystical union, or union with God.

But few individuals enter this kingdom of God, because few struggle to find it. As the Gita says:

Who cares to seek
For that perfect freedom?
One man, perhaps,
In many thousands.

Of course there are millions of Christians today who attend churches regularly and millions of Hindus and Buddhists who worship in temples and pagodas. But of those who do, few seek perfection in God. Most people are satisfied with living a more or less ethical life on earth in the hope of being rewarded in an afterlife for any good deeds they may have done. Christ's ideal of perfection is generally either forgotten or misunderstood. True, many people read the Sermon on the Mount, but few try to live its teachings. Most people argue whether one can find God, or whether perfection can be achieved or not, or what Christ meant by knowing the truth or seeing God. But this much I can say—that when Christ spoke to his disciples he meant literally that God could be seen in their present lives. And the disciples were hungering just for that truth, to know God, to be perfect even as the Father in heaven is perfect. How can a spiritual aspirant who is longing for the truth be satisfied with theology, with philosophy, with doctrines and creeds? Sri Ramakrishna used to tell the devotees: 'You have come to the mango garden. What good is it to count the leaves on the trees? Eat the mangoes and satisfy your hunger!' Similarly, Christ taught his disciples how to know God, how to realize him while living in the world. He did not state that divine perfection can be attained only after the death of the body.

If we go to the actual founders of the world's great religions we find that one truth expressed: realize God here and now! The great obstacle in the path of God-realization is mankind's laziness and lack of enthusiasm. Buddha called procrastination in the struggle for enlightenment the greatest sin. And Christ expressed the same idea when he said: 'No man, having put his hand to the plough, and looking back, is fit for the kingdom of God.'

There are several methods by which perfection in God may be reached. When perfection is achieved, every aspect of the aspirant's being is illumined. But it is natural for the methods, or paths to perfection, to focus certain tendencies in human character; for it is obvious that some people are thoughtful, some emotional, some active or contemplative, and that their spiritual practices should reflect their characters. In Vedanta, four main paths to the attainment of union with God are generally recognized. These paths, or yogas, are useful in clarifying the way to perfection as taught by Jesus.

In karma yoga, the path of selfless work, every action is offered to God as a sacrament. By dedicating the fruits of one's work to God, the spiritual aspirant eventually achieves purity of heart and attains union with God.

Jnana yoga is the path of discrimination between the eternal and the non-eternal. When by the process of elimination all transitory phenomena have been analysed and then rejected,

Brahman alone remains, and the spiritual aspirant realizes through meditation his union with the impersonal aspect of the Godhead.

Bhakti yoga is the path of devotion. In this path, the worshipper merges his ego in his chosen ideal of God by cultivating intense love for him as a personal being. The majority of believers in all the great religions of the world follow bhakti yoga.

Raja yoga is the path of formal meditation. It is the method of concentrating the mind one-pointedly on the supreme reality until complete absorption is attained. This path may be followed exclusively, often by those who lead predominantly contemplative lives. But, in a sense, raja yoga may be said to combine the other three paths, since meditation may include God-dedicated action, worship, discrimination, and concentration on the Chosen Ideal. Although a balanced spiritual life demands a harmonious combination of all four yogas, one or another usually predominates, depending on the temperament of the aspirant.

Among the teachings of Jesus, there are many which can be classified according to one or another of the yogas. For example, when Jesus said, 'Inasmuch as ye have done it unto the least of these my brethren, ye have done it unto me', he was teaching in the spirit of karma yoga, worship of God through service of man.

Discrimination between the real and the unreal, and renunciation of the unreal constitute the essence of jnana yoga. Jesus often taught discrimination and renunciation. For instance: '. . . lay up for yourselves treasures in heaven, where neither moth nor rust doth corrupt, and where thieves do not break through nor steal.' And 'Ye cannot serve God and mammon.'

The preliminary steps of raja yoga, the path of meditation, include abstention from harming others, from falsehood, from theft, from incontinence and greed, and observation of purity and devotion to God. Practice of these disciplines helps to make possible one-pointed concentration of the mind, meditation, and absorption in God. Jesus advocated the practice of these same disciplines. And he himself spent a great deal of time in meditation and absorption, often retiring into solitude for this purpose.

But of all the ways to union with God, Jesus emphasized most the way of devotion, reiterating the 'first and great commandment': 'Thou shalt love the Lord thy God with all thy heart, and with all thy soul, and with all thy mind.' Jesus' teachings on devotion—like those of other avatars—range from statements in which he regarded himself as a dualist, a devotee of God, to statements in which he asserted his identity with the Godhead. In the first clause of the Lord's Prayer (which will be discussed in greater detail in the next chapter) Jesus did not describe himself directly as God but spoke of him as another, teaching us to worship God as our Father in heaven. In numerous passages in the Gospel according to St John, Jesus made the point that love for the Son brings us the Father's love: 'If a man love me, he will keep my words: and my Father will love him, and we will come unto him, and make our abode with him.' 'For the Father himself loveth you, because ye have loved me, and have believed that I came out from God.' In other passages Jesus unequivocally declared his identity with the Father: 'I and my Father are one.' 'He that hath seen me hath seen the Father . . .' This identity is implied in teachings on devotion such as these: 'Abide in me, and I in you. As the branch cannot bear fruit of itself, except it abide in the vine; no more can ye, except ye abide in me.' 'Come unto me, all ye that labour and are heavy laden, and I will give you rest.'

Many spiritual teachers have stressed the practice of devotion, because it is the easiest path to God-realization. In this path the renunciation of the aspirant is entirely natural. He does not have to suppress a single one of his emotions. He only strives to intensify them and to direct them to God.

In the human heart there is the desire to love and be loved, to want the affection of a father, a mother, a friend, a sweetheart. But most of us do not recognize that this desire is really a desire for God disguised as something else. Ultimately in our human relationships we feel frustrated and alone, because the love we know and express on the human plane is merely an imperfect reflection of 'the real thing'. The Upanishads tell us:

'It is not for the sake of the wife that the wife is dear, but for the sake of the Self. It is not for the sake of the husband that the husband is dear, but for the sake of the Self. It is not for the sake of the children that the children are dear, but for the sake of the Self. . . . It is not for the sake of itself that anything whatever is esteemed, but for the sake of the Self.'

God's love attracts us, but we misread it. To read it truly, to find fulfilment of the desire for love is possible only when we turn our love towards God, who is love itself.

This does not mean that human love is wrong and should be avoided. Through human love such qualities as compassion and unselfishness are developed and experiences necessary for spiritual unfoldment are gained. Human affection need not be forcibly renounced; it becomes spiritualized when it is given unselfishly, without possessiveness or bargaining for return.

One who aspires to union with God must know that all the existing religious sects revere one and the same Reality. A Hindu prayer says: 'They call you by so many names. They divide you, as it were, by different names. Yet in each one of these you manifest your omnipotence. . . . You reach the worshipper through any of them.' God has infinite aspects and expressions. He may reveal himself to his devotee as personal or impersonal, with or without form. Therefore the aspirant must never criticize any one of the many religious paths and practices that lead to God. But this does not mean that he can follow one divine ideal today and another tomorrow. The tender plant of spirituality must be protected until it grows into a sturdy tree. In order that the mind may become absorbed in God, the follower of bhakti yoga practises devotion to a single ideal. When love for his Chosen Ideal illumines his heart, the devotee will realize that it is his ideal whom others worship under different names and forms; then he will love God in all his aspects.

Many followers of the path of devotion choose a divine incarnation as their ideal, whom they adore as one with the indwelling Self and the transcendent reality. To quote Swami Vivekananda:

'. . . perfect men are instinctively worshipped as God in every country. They are the most perfect manifestations of the eternal Self. That is why men worship incarnations such as Christ or Buddha.

'It is true that you and I, and the poorest of us, the meanest even, embody that God, even reflect that God. The vibration of light is everywhere, omnipresent; but . . . the omnipresent God of the universe cannot be seen until he is reflected by these giant lamps of the earth—the Prophets, the man-Gods, the Incarnations, the embodiments of God. Our Scriptures say, "These great children of Light, who manifest the Light themselves, who are Light themselves, they being worshipped, become, as it were, one with us and we become one with them." '

Thus the great prophets and sons of God, being worshipped, lead mankind to freedom and perfection. They are always aware that this is their mission, and they proclaim it to all. Jesus says: 'I am the light of the world: he that followeth me shall not walk in darkness, but shall have the light of life.' Sri Krishna says: 'Lay down all duties in me, your refuge. Fear no longer, for I will save you from sin and from bondage.' Sri Ramakrishna says: 'I am the sanctuary.' 'Give me the power of attorney; I will release you from all bonds of karma.'

To take refuge in such a teacher is to take refuge in God, which means that we must centre our life in him. God's grace is already upon us; but in order that we may feel his grace the heart must be purified. And in order that the heart may be purified we must practise spiritual disciplines:

First, wherever the unruly senses and mind wander, we must try to see the Lord. We read in one of the Vedanta

scriptures: 'By gathering pure food, the heart is purified.'
'Food' here means whatever impressions are received through
the five senses. The secret of this spiritual discipline, then, is
to cover everything with the presence of God.

Second, we are to practise the ethical virtues taught in the
scriptures—virtues such as compassion, non-violence, and
chastity.

Finally, we must set aside regular hours for the exclusive
practice of prayer and worship. Worship means holding the
chosen ideal of Godhead before you as an object of love, and
in his living presence to direct your thoughts uninterruptedly
towards him, like oil poured from one vessel to another for a
long time. Prayer, in the words of St Paul, is to be offered
'without ceasing'.

Through the practice of these disciplines, constant recollectedness of God awakens in the devotee's heart. The thought
of his beloved Lord is continually in his consciousness. All
cravings leave him. Only one desire remains: to love God and
live in complete self-surrender to his will. This pure and selfless devotion is followed by absorption in God, and ultimate
union with him. Love, lover, and beloved become one. The
effects of this supreme love are described by the sage Narada
in his aphorisms on bhakti yoga:

'Obtaining which, man becomes perfect, immortal, satisfied; he
desires nothing, grieves not, hates none, does not delight in
sense objects, becomes intoxicated—rejoices in the bliss of the
Atman.'

The man who experiences this unitary consciousness enters
into the kingdom of heaven and becomes perfect even as the
Father in heaven is perfect.

*Take heed that ye do not your alms before men, to be seen
of them: otherwise ye have no reward of your Father which is
in heaven.*

Therefore when thou doest thine alms, do not sound a

*trumpet before thee, as the hypocrites do in the synagogues
and in the streets, that they may have glory of men. Verily I
say unto you, They have their reward.*

*But when thou doest alms, let not thy left hand know what
thy right hand doeth:*

*That thine alms may be in secret: and thy Father which
seeth in secret himself shall reward thee openly.*

Here Jesus speaks of action and its reward, cause and effect,
which in Vedanta is set forth as the law of karma. The law of
karma states that if I do some good deed for you, I will get my
reward. Whether you yourself give me that reward or not does
not matter. If I do good, I shall receive good in return. If I do
something bad, bad will come back to me. That is the law.
(St Paul says in his Epistle to the Galatians: '. . . whatsoever
a man soweth, that shall he also reap.') But in order that we
may reach perfection, we must free ourselves from all attachment, from all craving for the fruits of action. We must free
the mind from every kind of impression and tendency—the
good as well as the bad, for good actions also create karma. If
we want to transcend karma, the Gita teaches, we must learn
to offer the fruits of our work to God. This is karma yoga—
the way to union with God through God-dedicated action.

In karma yoga, the devotee's whole life becomes an unend-
ing ritual since every action is performed, not in the hope of
one's personal gain or advantage but as worship. To dedicate
the fruits of one's work to God is to work with non-attachment. We must not give way to pride and vanity if the results of our work are successful and win popular praise. On
the other hand, having done our best, we must not despair if
our work has disappointing results, or is harshly criticized, or
disregarded altogether. Many men and women will work to
the best of their ability in a dedicated manner. But if their
ideal is anything short of union with God, it will be almost
impossible for them not to despair if they find their cause de-
feated and their life-work brought to nothing. Only the de-

votee of God need never despair because he renounces the fruits of action. He has his reward—God himself.

To many people, non-attachment suggests indifference, laziness, and fatalism. Actually, non-attachment is the very opposite of indifference. It is a positive virtue, born of attachment to God. In fact, the follower of karma yoga must be intensely attached to his work while he is doing it. His whole mind must be concentrated on doing it perfectly since it is to be offered as worship. But he must be able to detach himself at a moment's notice. Through the practice of non-attachment and selfless service the devotee frees himself from the wheel of cause and effect, deed and reward, and obtains the Infinite.

And when thou prayest, thou shalt not be as the hypocrites are: for they love to pray standing in the synagogues and in the corners of the streets, that they may be seen of men. Verily I say unto you, They have their reward.

But thou, when thou prayest, enter into thy closet, and when thou hast shut thy door, pray to thy Father which is in secret; and thy Father which seeth in secret shall reward thee openly.

Here Christ begins his instructions on prayer. He tells us that if we want anything less than God, we can have it. If we want a reputation for holiness, we can go out into some public place and pray where everybody can see us. And we can get our reward—no doubt about it. Public prayer receives public rewards—recognition, wealth, followers, and power.

But true religion is not a matter for display. It is something very sacred, and therefore secret. This is why Christ warns us not to make a show of worship. Genuine purity and spirituality need no advertising. If you pray to God for his own sake —not to make him the means to some other end, but wanting him alone—then never mind the world, never mind whether it blames or admires you. Go apart into a secret place and ask for him. You can be certain that he will give himself to you.

He will reward you with his own presence.

But when ye pray, use not vain repetitions, as the heathen do: for they think that they shall be heard for their much speaking.
Be not ye therefore like unto them: for your Father knoweth what things ye have need of, before ye ask him.

God is not deceived. He knows our needs and our innermost thoughts. He is the Hearer behind the ear, the Thinker behind the mind, the Speaker behind the tongue. He is that Pure Consciousness whose reflection upon our intellect makes us conscious. He knows whether our prayers are hypocritical—'vain repetitions'—or the supplications of a sincere heart. Sri Ramakrishna used to say:

'When mind and speech unite in earnest prayer, that prayer is answered. Of no avail are the prayers of the man who says with his lips, "These are all Thine, O Lord!" and at the same time thinks in his heart that all of them are his. Don't be a traitor to your thoughts! . . . Pray with a sincere and simple heart, and your prayers will be heard.'

CHAPTER V

The Lord's Prayer

MATTHEW 6:9-13

After this manner therefore pray ye:

HAVING instructed us how to pray, Christ now gives us an actual prayer which we may use—the Lord's Prayer. It is perhaps the best known prayer in the world, and many people repeat it every day of their lives. Like all great statements, this prayer is both simple and profound; and if we take it literally, we can miss its deeper significance. Its meaning is revealed to those who practise spiritual disciplines, for it gives in brief form the fundamental principles upon which a holy life must be based. Each phrase of the prayer serves as a reminder of the ideal and the methods already presented.

Two basic types of prayer are used by different individuals: man-centred and God-centred prayer. People whose prayer is man-centred beseech God to enrich their life on earth, to remove their sufferings, to provide them with wealth, success, and comfort. God-centred prayer, on the other hand, is motivated by spiritual discrimination and devotion. People whose prayers are God-centred seek Him alone, knowing that God-realization is the whole purpose of life. The Lord's Prayer is God-centred, and in it Jesus teaches us how to become absorbed in the consciousness of God and find eternal joy and freedom. Anyone who sincerely seeks God can approach him with the Lord's Prayer. He does not have to subscribe to any religious creed or dogma. If he accepts the idea that God exists and can be realized, and he follows Christ's teachings, he will reach perfection.

The Prayer begins, *Our Father . . .*

Christ is teaching us how to think of God when we pray to him. For most of us, God as an impersonal being is too abstract to meditate upon. He is an idea, it seems, while we feel that we are flesh and blood, with emotions and desires. Therefore, as we saw in the previous chapter, Christ, like other great spiritual teachers, emphasized the path of devotion, in which God is worshipped as a personal being. In order that we may love the Lord with all our heart, soul, and mind, as Christ wants us to do, we have to consider him our very own. And in order that we may consider him our very own, we have to enter into a definite relationship with him.

The different expressions of love which exist on the human plane also exist on the divine plane. A Hindu prayer says: 'Thou art our loving mother; thou art our compassionate father; thou art our true friend and constant companion. Thou art our only treasure and our only wisdom. Thou art all in all.' We must begin with a specific relationship with God; later we come to the understanding that he is all in all.

According to the Hindu teachers of bhakti yoga, there are five chief relationships with God: first, the relationship between creature and Creator; second, between servant and Master or child and Parent; third, friend and Friend; fourth, parent and Child; and fifth, the relationship between wife and Husband, or lover (seen as feminine) and Beloved.

The five relationships with God are not confined to Hindu worship, for Christians also have long been familiar with them. Hindu devotees adore the baby Krishna; Christians adore the Christ child. Brother Lawrence looked on himself primarily as a servant of the Lord. Catholic nuns consider themselves to be brides of Christ, and even wear wedding bands to indicate their state. Christ himself taught the attitude of friendship with God. He said to his disciples (John 15:14-15):

'Ye are my friends, if ye do whatsoever I command you. Henceforth I call you not servants; . . . but I have called you friends;

for all things that I have heard of my Father I have made known unto you.'

In the Lord's Prayer, however, and in many other of Christ's teachings, we are told to think of God as our Father, whom we may regard partly with reverence, but chiefly with trust, absolute confidence, and love. We are under his protection. We are safe with him.

which art in heaven . . .

Christ tells us that our Father is in heaven. In every age people ask for proof of the existence of God. Clever demonstrations have been devised by philosophers and logicians, establishing God as a 'necessary proposition'. Yet every argument substantiating God's existence has been contradicted by the arguments of opposing philosophers and logicians. In the long run, there is only one way to verify the actuality of God, and that is to see him for oneself. All attempts to arrive at a proof by means of reasoning are futile, because what we are trying to establish is only the existence of our *idea* of God. Hence, even if we could possibly make such a proof, how could we guarantee that our idea and the reality of God would correspond? Standing in our present position, far inland, we cannot prove the existence of the ocean; we cannot even be certain that our idea of that ocean corresponds in any way to the reality. An experienced traveller will advise us: 'Take that road, go to the top of that hill. Then you will see the ocean itself, and you will not need any further verification.'

During the course of the world's history many great illumined teachers have told us: 'God exists. I know, because I have seen him.' The only question that remains for us is: do we believe them? If after watching their lives and learning all that can be known about them we feel that these men are trustworthy, then conviction will begin to grow in our own hearts also. And, when once we have the beginning of that conviction, it will be our own fault if we do not try to find certainty by starting along the road which those men have travelled, in order that we, like them, may reach the hilltop and see the infinite ocean of bliss for ourselves.

We are told to seek the Father 'in heaven'. But where is heaven? Both Christianity and Vedanta teach—as I have pointed out in the previous chapter—that the kingdom of heaven is within us. This does not mean that heaven has a spatial existence. Heaven is beyond space. To be 'in heaven' is to realize God in our own consciousness. When we begin to look within, however, we do not see heaven, for earth is also within us. Blinded by ignorance of our divine nature, we see only earth. Earth-consciousness is our physical consciousness, our consciousness of time, space, and relativity. Conversely, heaven is that which abides forever, the kingdom of God. As long as the mind is impure, as long as it is attached to the objects of this world, we are conscious of earth. When this same mind is purified through prayer and worship, it realizes the Father which is in heaven. My master used to say: 'With the eye of the senses, what will a man see but matter? And with the eye of the spirit, what will he see but spirit?' From the experiences of illumined souls we learn that at the time of God-realization, in the superconscious state of samadhi, there is no awareness of the physical world. That is because the saint has gone beyond time, space, and relativity. But because we cannot have this superconsciousness all in a moment, we should begin by thinking of God as dwelling within our hearts, and praying to him there. Brother Lawrence said: 'We must make our heart a spiritual temple wherein to adore Him incessantly. . . . He is within us; seek Him not elsewhere.'

Hallowed be thy name.

Christ here puts emphasis upon the name of God, the Logos, the Word. In the avatar, as we have seen, the Word is made flesh. But the name of God in itself is of the greatest religious significance. Both the Old and the New Testaments set forth the spiritual practice of hallowing God's name: 'O magnify

the Lord with me, and let us exalt his name together' (Psalms).
'. . . let us offer the sacrifice of praise to God continually, that
is, the fruit of our lips giving thanks to his name' (Hebrews).
'For whosoever shall call upon the name of the Lord shall be
saved' (Romans). And in the Gospel according to St John we
read that Jesus asked his disciples to pray in his name: 'Verily,
verily, I say unto you, Whatsoever ye shall ask the Father in
my name, he will give it you. Hitherto ye have asked nothing
in my name: ask, and ye shall receive, that your joy may be
full.'

In India we find the same idea accepted which is expressed
at the beginning of the Fourth Gospel, that God and his name
are one. In Vedanta, God's name is called the mantra. There
are various mantras, depending on the particular aspect of God
a devotee chooses to worship. The teacher gives his disciple the
mantra at the ceremony of initiation, and enjoins him to keep
it sacred and secret and to meditate upon the aspect of God
which it represents for the rest of his life. The essence of the
disciple's Chosen Ideal is concentrated in the mantra in the
form of a sound-symbol. As the name of God is repeated, the
spiritual power with which it is charged becomes evident. By
hallowing the name over and over again, we let God take possession of our conscious minds so that finally, no matter what
we are doing or saying or thinking, some part of our minds
will be praising him.

One of India's greatest saints, Sri Chaitanya, taught his
followers to rely heavily on this simple and effective method of
remembering God:

> Chant the Name of the Lord and his glory unceasingly,
> That the mirror of the heart may be wiped clean
> And quenched that mighty forest fire,
> Worldly lust, raging furiously within.

> Oh Name, stream down in moonlight on the lotus-heart,
> Opening its cup to knowledge of thyself.
> Oh self, drown deep in the waves of his bliss,
> Chanting his name continually,

Tasting his nectar at every step,
Bathing in his name, that bath for weary souls.

Various are thy names, Oh Lord,
In each and every name thy power resides.
No times are set, no rites are needful,
    for chanting of thy name,
So vast is thy mercy.
How huge, then, is my wretchedness
Who find, in this empty life and heart,
No devotion to thy name!

The practice of repeating the name of God over and over again is also taught in Catholicism: 'Hail Mary' is a mantra. The Jesus Prayer, a form of Mantra, is recognized in the Eastern Orthodox Church. Its practice is explained in two remarkable books, *The Way of a Pilgrim* and its sequel *The Pilgrim Continues His Way*, which record the spiritual pilgrimage of a Russian devotee in the nineteenth century:

'The continuous interior Prayer of Jesus is a constant uninterrupted calling upon the divine Name of Jesus with the lips, in the spirit, in the heart; while forming a mental picture of his constant presence, and imploring his grace during every occupation, at all times, in all places, even during sleep. The appeal is couched in these terms, "Lord Jesus Christ, have mercy on me". One who accustoms himself to this appeal experiences as a result so deep a consolation and so great a need to offer the prayer always, that he can no longer live without it, and it will continue to voice itself within him of its own accord. . . .

'Many so-called enlightened people regard this frequent offering of one and the same prayer as useless and even trifling, calling it mechanical and a thoughtless occupation of simple people. But unfortunately they do not know the secret which is revealed as a result of this mechanical exercise, they do not know how this frequent service of the lips imperceptibly becomes a genuine appeal of the heart, sinks down into the inward life, becomes a delight, becomes, as it were, natural to the soul, bringing it light and nourishment and leading it on to union with God.'

Psychologically speaking, how does this method of reliance on a mantra work? Suppose you had the problem of cleaning a dirty ink bottle that is fastened to a table. You cannot take the bottle up and empty the ink out. But you can pour clean water in and so force the ink and dirt to overflow. You keep on pouring in the clean water until all the ink has been washed out and the bottle contains nothing but clear water. In the same way, it is not possible to empty the mind of its worldly cravings and attachments by throwing away the contents of consciousness and making the mind blank. But what we can do is pour the clear water of the thought of God into our minds until all the dirt has been washed away. Through repetition of the mantra, mind and heart are purified. Eventually the name is experienced as living and conscious, as one with God—and illumination is attained.

I once met an Indian monk who had achieved illumination by the sole spiritual practice of hallowing God's name. When I was a college student, I visited Brindavan. There I learned about a holy man who lived in a forest nearby, and I decided to go and see him. A narrow path led me to a small hut in the centre of a clearing. Soon the holy man came out of the hut, sat on a mat which his disciple spread on the ground, and motioned me to be seated also. There was a tangible atmosphere of saintliness about him. I prostrated before him. Then I asked, 'Revered sir, how did you attain this state?' 'Nama,' he said, giving me to understand that he had achieved perfection through repetition of the nama, the Lord's name. He said no more, and I sat before him in silence for a while. At last I bowed down to him and left. My heart was filled with peace.

Thy kingdom come.

When a Hindu performs the ritualistic worship, the first

prayer he says is: 'As with eyes wide open a man sees the sky above him, so the seers see always the Supreme Truth, God, the all-pervading Existence.' If only our divine sight opens we shall see God's kingdom existent here. This is not a hope for the future. Lazy Christians say: 'O Lord, some day I will go to heaven and live in your company,' just as lazy Hindus say: 'Some day, in some incarnation, I will realize God.' But Christ tells us that God's kingdom has come already; it has always been with us, and we must realize this. At least when we pray and meditate we should forget this universe, forget ourselves, and feel that God alone exists. Through such practice, our ignorance will vanish one day, and we will actually see his kingdom in our hearts and all around us.

Thy will be done in earth, as it is in heaven.

How is a spiritual aspirant to do the will of God? How can he possibly know if what he is doing is God's will or not? Throughout history, in every country, we find all sorts of people doing exactly what they want to do and claiming that it is God's will. But, until we become spiritually illumined, until God actually speaks to us, we cannot know, in any given situation, what his will may be. When the day comes that brings us into perfect union with him, so that we are literally filled with God, then we can become his instruments and do his will. But even in our present ignorance, we can say with confidence that God's will is whatever will lead us to him. And we can pray: 'Lord, I don't know what your will is, but guide me so that I may do it. May I be a tool in your hand!'

Give us this day our daily bread.

'Our daily bread' is the bread of divine grace, and we are praying that this grace may be revealed to us now, 'this day', this moment, and forever.

As a child, I used to be very fond of the story of a young girl who went into the woods where, she had been told, God could be seen. And there she waited for him. She was firmly convinced that sooner or later he would pass her way. She became a woman and then an old woman. In all that time God had not come, but she went on waiting eagerly, ready for him at every moment of every day. At last God did really come. He passed by her, and she saw him, and her whole life was blessed.

That is the faith we need: we must know that God's grace may be revealed to us at any moment, yet at the same time we must be prepared to wait patiently. Few people have learned to live in the expectancy of imminent grace. Most of us feel that we have so many impurities, so many faults to overcome, so much discipline to work through, that we cannot possibly reach God until some distant point in the future. This seeming humility is actually vanity, because it presupposes that we can know God through our own efforts, our own will power. That is all nonsense! Our own struggles will never make us pure or bring us the sight of God. No one can buy God with spiritual practices. The great souls who have attained illumination tell us that enlightenment comes only through divine grace.

In the Katha Upanishad we read:

'The Self is not known through study of the scriptures, nor through subtlety of the intellect, nor through much learning. Whom the Self chooses, by him is he attained. Verily unto him does the Self reveal his true being.'

Similarly, Christ declared: 'Ye have not chosen me, but I have chosen you . . .' This means that grace is necessary, but does it mean that God is partial? Swami Turiyananda, who was asked this question one day, answered:

'The Lord is not partial. His grace falls equally upon saint and sinner, just as rain falls on all the land. But only the ground which is cultivated, produces a good harvest.'

And Sri Ramakrishna used to say: 'The breeze of grace is

always blowing. Set your sail to catch that breeze.' This means that God's grace is always upon us; but self-effort and spiritual disciplines are necessary in order that we may become receptive to it. Christ said:

'Watch ye therefore: for ye know not when the master of the house cometh . . . Lest coming suddenly he find you sleeping.'

We must be watchful; we must struggle to fix the mind on God in prayer and meditation. But at the same time we should know that, quite irrespective of our efforts, through his grace he may reveal himself at any moment. We must always be ready.

And forgive us our debts, as we forgive our debtors.

A Hindu or a Buddhist would read the 'debts' in this passage as the debts of karma. The word karma stands for a mental or physical act and its consequences. Any thought we think, any action we perform has two consequences: first, it creates an impression in the mind, which means that we are sowing a seed for similar thoughts and actions in the future; second, it brings, according to the nature of the thought or deed, either happiness or misery. By our actions and reactions we are always contracting debts, obligations that must be paid off. We alone are responsible for these obligations. We are even responsible for our own character, which has resulted from our habits of thought and action. When we recognize our debts, when we realize that everything, good or bad, that comes to us, has been previously earned by ourselves alone, then we know that we must not hold anybody else responsible for anything that we suffer. We all have a tendency to accuse others for whatever in our life may go wrong. At the beginning of creation we find Adam blaming Eve for their fall; and Eve, in her turn, blaming the serpent. If we are ready to assume responsibility for our own karma and not blame others, then it will be easy for us to forgive those in debt to us, those who take something away from us or do us some harm. Only when we have this forgiveness in our hearts can we expect forgiveness from God.

What binds us to the law of karma, the law of cause and effect? Our sense of ego, which makes us feel separate from God. In the Svetasvatara Upanishad we read:

'This vast universe is a wheel. Upon it are all creatures that are subject to birth, death, and rebirth. Round and round it turns, and never stops. It is the wheel of Brahman. As long as the individual self thinks it is separate from Brahman, it revolves upon the wheel in bondage to the laws of birth, death, and rebirth. But when through the grace of Brahman it realizes its identity with him, it revolves upon the wheel no longer. It achieves immortality.'

In order to free ourselves from the bondage of karma we must offer the fruits of our actions to the Lord and surrender our sense of ego to him. We must pray to God for forgiveness of our debts so that, through his grace, we may transcend karma and reach union with him.

And lead us not into temptation, but deliver us from evil: For thine is the kingdom, and the power, and the glory, for ever. Amen.

Many persons find this part of the Lord's Prayer difficult to understand. How is it possible, they ask, for God to tempt anybody? Some scholars, concluding that Jesus could not have spoken these words, have gone back to the ancient original texts to make new translations, hoping thereby to arrive at a meaning more consistent with their understanding of Christ's gospel. But to the student of Vedanta, the Prayer is meaningful just as we find it here. Is not the whole universe one gigantic temptation? God himself has conjured up the magic of creation, preservation, and destruction through maya, his cosmic power, which is the basis of the universe of mind and

matter. Fascinated by maya, man does not see that God, the
Atman, dwells within his own heart. He sees instead the mani-
fold universe and wants to enjoy its objects and attractions
through his outgoing senses. Forgetting God, he becomes a
slave to the temptation of God's maya and lives in bondage to
ignorance and the cravings of his ego. The process which takes
place when man succumbs to temptation is described in the
Gita :

'Thinking about sense-objects will attach you to sense-objects;
grow attached, and you become addicted; thwart your ad-
diction, it turns to anger; be angry and you confuse your mind;
confuse your mind, you forget the lesson of experience; forget
experience, you lose discrimination; lose discrimination, and
you miss life's only purpose.'

The Vedantist sees an allegory of the temptation of maya in
the story of the Garden of Eden. Adam symbolizes the Atman,
the divine Self; Eve, the intellect of Adam; the serpent, maya.
As Eve (the intellect) yields to temptation, Adam also succumbs: he too eats of the forbidden fruit. He forgets his divine
nature, recognizes good and evil, and experiences, instead of
Paradise, the universe of time, space and relativity.

Sri Ramakrishna used to pray to God as the Divine Mother,
and in his prayer he recognized God's temptation :

'I take refuge at thy hallowed feet. . . . Please grant me, Mother,
that I, thy child, may not be deluded by thy world-bewitching
maya.'

He often compared the Divine Mother to an earthly mother
who gives toys to her child. A mother goes about her house-
hold tasks as long as her child is happy with his toys. But
when he tires of play and cries for her, she drops her work,
runs to him, and takes him in her arms. As long as we are
satisfied busying ourselves with the things of this world, the
Divine Mother lets us play. But as soon as we turn away from

her creation and become restless for her, she graciously reveals herself to us.

In order to escape from maya and regain our freedom and perfection, we must restrain the outgoing senses and turn within, where God dwells; we must take refuge in God and pray for divine grace. Sri Krishna says: 'How hard to break through is this my maya . . . ! But he who takes refuge within me only shall pass beyond maya, he and no other.'

When we pass beyond maya and God becomes revealed, then we see that 'From Joy springs this universe, in Joy exists this universe, and unto Joy goes back this universe'. We experience God everywhere, within every creature and object, and we recognize that his is 'the kingdom, and the power, and the glory, for ever'.

CHAPTER VI

God and Mammon

MATTHEW 6:14-34

*For if ye forgive men their trespasses, your heavenly Father
will also forgive you:*
*But if ye forgive not men their trespasses, neither will your
Father forgive your trespasses.*

UNTIL we become established in the virtue of forgiveness, we
cannot attain the purity of heart which enables us to see God.
The practice of forgiveness is therefore of fundamental im-
portance for the spiritual aspirant. In the Sermon on the
Mount, as we have seen, Christ stresses this practice repeatedly.
He teaches mercy, reconciliation, and forgiveness of debts. But
besides the Sermon, the Gospels record many instances of
Christ's teaching of forgiveness, both by precept and by his
own example. When Peter asked him, 'Lord, how oft shall my
brother sin against me, and I forgive him? till seven times?'
Christ answered, 'I say not unto thee, Until seven times: but
Until seventy times seven'.

Christ never condemned those who had wronged others—
or himself. He would bless them, saying, 'Go and sin no more',
'Thy sins are forgiven'. And in his prayer on the cross he asked
the Father to pardon the ignorance of men, 'for they know
not what they do'.

All great spiritual teachers have emphasized the importance
of forgiveness in spiritual life. Buddha said:

'If a man foolishly does me wrong, I will return to him the protection of my ungrudging love; the more evil comes from him,

the more good shall go from me . . . Cleanse your heart of malice and cherish no hatred, not even against your enemies; but embrace all living beings with kindness.'

These teachers agree that if we lack forgiveness, if we hold thoughts of anger or hatred, we will cause misery for ourselves as well as for others. They advise us to raise opposite waves of thought—thoughts of love and compassion—so that we will be at peace with the world and ourselves.

Why is it so difficult for most of us to follow the teaching of forgiveness? Because when someone cherishes ill will towards us we react by feeling hurt. And what is hurt the most? The ego. Forgiveness is perhaps the greatest of all virtues; because if we can truly forgive men their trespasses we rise above the ego, which obstructs our vision of God.

Moreover when ye fast, be not, as the hypocrites, of a sad countenance: for they disfigure their faces, that they may appear unto men to fast. Verily I say unto you, They have their reward.

But thou, when thou fastest, anoint thine head, and wash thy face;

That thou appear not unto men to fast, but unto thy Father which is in secret: and thy Father, which seeth in secret, shall reward thee openly.

A traditional Hindu saying warns: 'Beware of these: the man who wears a sacred leaf on his ear, one who is secretive and does not talk at all, one who cannot keep a secret and talks too much, a woman with a double veil, and the water of a pond which is covered with scum.' In other words, beware of things which are other than they seem. A man who makes a show of religion has no religion at all. If a man sincerely yearns for God-vision, he will be rewarded by his Father 'which seeth in secret', by the Lord who dwells in his inmost heart. Such a man, finding religion inside, will be too humble to display it outside: he keeps it sacred within himself.

Furthermore, spirituality and sadness do not go together.

Yoga Psychology explains that the practice of religious disciplines purifies the mind. And the purified mind—as we read in one of Patanjali's aphorisms—loses all lethargy and moroseness (tamas) and becomes established in cheerfulness (sattva). Commenting on this aphorism, Swami Vivekananda said:

'The first sign that you are becoming religious is that you are becoming cheerful. When a man is gloomy, that may be dyspepsia, but it is not religion. A pleasurable feeling is the nature of sattva. Everything is pleasurable to the sattvic man, and when this experience comes, know that you are progressing in yoga. . . . To the yogi, everything is bliss, every human face that he sees brings cheerfulness to him. That is a sign of a virtuous man. Misery is caused by sin and by no other cause. What business have you with clouded faces? . . . If you have a clouded face, do not go out that day, shut yourself up in your room. What right have you to carry this disease out into the world?'

God is love and bliss—the very opposite of sadness. A man who keeps his mind in God will be flooded with joy. Thus we read in a monastic breviary: 'Joyful let us drink the sober drunkenness of the Spirit!'

Lay not up for yourselves treasures upon earth, where moth and rust doth corrupt, and where thieves break through and steal:

But lay up for yourselves treasures in heaven, where neither moth nor rust doth corrupt, and where thieves do not break through nor steal.

For where your treasure is, there will your heart be also.

Here Jesus is repeating what we have heard already, that one of the most important conditions for successfully starting to live the spiritual life is to have right discrimination—discrimination between the eternal and the non-eternal. The more this faculty is cultivated, the more we lose our thirst for the ephemeral treasures of the objective world and turn towards the infinite and eternal treasures of heaven. The philosopher Spinoza defined this spiritual discrimination as follows:

'For the things which men, to judge by their actions, deem the highest good, are riches, fame, or sensual pleasure. Of these, the last is followed by satiety and repentance, the other two are never satiated; the more we have, the more we want; while the love of fame compels us to order our lives by the opinions of others. But if a thing is not loved, no quarrels will arise concerning it, no sadness will be felt if it perishes, no envy if another has it, in short, no disturbances of the mind. All these spring from the love of that which passes away. But the love of a thing eternal and infinite fills the mind wholly with joy, and is unmingled with sadness. Therefore it is greatly to be desired, and to be sought with all our strength.'

The purpose of life, in the words of the Upanishads, is 'to attain abiding bliss in the midst of the fleeting pleasures of life'. And that abiding bliss is the bliss of God. To be merged in the consciousness of God is to enter into his kingdom.

Many of us understand intellectually that the purpose of life is to realize God and that worldly pleasures exist only for the moment. Yet our hearts do not respond, because we have formed the habit of finding pleasure in sense objects. Now we have to create the new habit of finding joy in God. Brother Lawrence said:

'In order to know God, we must often think of him; and when we come to love him, we shall then also think of him often: for our heart will be with our treasure.'

In other words, once we have decided that we want treasures in heaven, and not treasures upon earth, we must learn to fix our hearts in God. No matter how often we may show weakness and forget to practise recollectedness, we shall reach the goal in the end as long as we keep up the attempt. A little

baby tries to walk: as one watches him falling down continually, it seems incredible that he will ever succeed. But he
picks himself up, again and again, because the urge within
him is so strong; and in the end he can walk upright without
faltering. Similarly, there is no failure in the spiritual life, as
long as we do not give up the struggle. And we shall never
give it up once we have become firmly convinced in heart and
mind that God is our only treasure.

The light of the body is the eye: if therefore thine eye be
single, thy whole body shall be full of light.
But if thine eye be evil, thy whole body shall be full of dark-
ness. If therefore the light that is in thee be darkness, how
great is that darkness!

In order for us to fix our hearts in the eternal and to renounce the ephemeral objects of the world, our eyes must be
'single'. We must not run after this or that object, but must
concentrate with one-pointed devotion upon God. For the
attainment of illumination, says the Gita,

'the will is directed singly towards one ideal. When a man
lacks this discrimination, his will wanders in all directions,
after innumerable aims.'

As long as a man lacks spiritual discrimination his 'whole body
shall be full of darkness'. He continues to live in ignorance,
and the true Self, the divine light within him, remains covered.
Concentration of the mind on the chosen ideal of God is the
way to uncover that divine light.

This concentration, then, purifies what enters the consciousness through the senses. 'The light of the body is the eye,' says
Christ, comparing the eye to a window through which the outside world enters. Through the five senses we gather impressions, and the sum total of these impressions make up our
character. If we see good, we take in good; if we see evil, we
take in evil. As a Vedic prayer says, 'With our ears may

we hear what is good. With our eyes may we behold thy righteousness.' Wherever we look, instead of the names and forms of things, we must learn to see God, the all-pervading Spirit. In this way, rather than distracting us from our ideal, every object in the universe becomes an aid to God-realization.

And so the light of God pours in upon us until eventually our 'whole body shall be full of light'. The scriptures speak of great souls whose inner illumination became objectively visible; their bodies actually became full of light. Once I had the memorable privilege of witnessing such a transfiguration. It was in Banaras in October of 1914. Swami Premananda, who as a disciple of Ramakrishna had attained God-realization, used to visit various temples after taking his daily bath in the Ganges. I would accompany him. One day, after we finished worship in the temple of Annapurna, the Divine Mother, the head priest placed a garland of marigolds around Swami Premananda's neck. When the Swami was about to take the garland off to give it to me, I placed my palms together, bowed before him and said: 'No, holy sir, please keep the garland yourself. You look so beautiful!' The word 'beautiful' reminded the Swami of God's beauty, and he went into ecstasy. His face flushed, and then a light began to emanate from his whole body. Walking slowly, he left the temple, and I followed him. The temple lane was crowded as usual, but on either side of us people stared at the Swami and made way. It was quite evident that everyone present saw him illumined. We continued to walk through the streets of Banaras while crowds stood still, silently watching Swami Premananda. He was completely absorbed in the thought of God and oblivious of his surroundings. As we approached the outer gate of our monastery, Swami Nirbharananda, the abbot, saw us from the veranda. He immediately ordered the monks to prepare a special welcome for Swami Premananda. We entered the monastery grounds to the sound of gongs and conch shells, and the ringing of bells. Then, when we arrived at the veranda, Swami Premananda took the garland off and placed it around the neck of the abbot. Gradually the ecstasy abated, and the divine light disappeared.

No man can serve two masters: for either he will hate the one, and love the other; or else he will hold to the one, and despise the other. Ye cannot serve God and mammon.

Compare Christ's words with the Hindu saying about Rama, one of the avatars: 'Where Rama is, there is no worldly craving; and where worldly craving exists, Rama is not.' Let us face the facts: the attempt to serve 'God and mammon' simultaneously is quite hopeless. The great spiritual teachers tell us that it cannot be done. We cannot become absorbed in God as long as we are slaves to cravings such as lust and greed. Spiritual discrimination must accompany spiritual practices. When our discrimination ripens, renunciation follows as a matter of course. Then, like the merchant in Christ's parable, we will sell all our possessions in order to buy the 'one pearl of great price', which is the kingdom of heaven.

A reading of Christ's gospel makes it obvious that he taught the ideal of renunciation exactly as it has been taught by all the great seers of truth: If you really want God, you must give up mammon. Like the message of Rama, Krishna, Buddha, and every other avatar, Christ's message is universal: spiritual life without renunciation is impossible. In his own words:

'If any man will come after me, let him deny himself, and take up his cross, and follow me. For whosoever will save his life shall lose it: and whosoever will lose his life for my sake shall find it. For what is a man profited, if he shall gain the whole world, and lose his own soul? or what shall a man give in exchange for his soul?'

What does it really mean to deny yourself, to renounce? It does not mean escape from the world and its duties. It means giving up selfishness, the sense of 'me' and 'mine'. It means loving God with all one's heart, soul, and mind. Sri Ramakrishna used to say: 'Why does the lover of God renounce everything for the sake of Him whom he loves? The moth after seeing a light does not return to darkness; the ant dies in the heap of sugar but does not turn back. So the lover of God gladly sacrifices his life for the attainment of divine bliss, caring for nothing else.'

Therefore I say unto you, Take no thought for your life, what ye shall eat, or what ye shall drink; nor yet for your body, what ye shall put on. Is not the life more than meat, and the body than raiment?

Behold the fowls of the air: for they sow not, neither do they reap, nor gather into barns; yet your heavenly Father feedeth them. Are ye not much better than they?

Which of you by taking thought can add one cubit unto his stature?

And why take ye thought for raiment? Consider the lilies of the field, how they grow; they toil not, neither do they spin:

And yet I say unto you, That even Solomon in all his glory was not arrayed like one of these.

Wherefore, if God so clothe the grass of the field, which to day is, and to morrow is cast into the oven, shall he not much more clothe you, O ye of little faith?

Millions of people have known these words since their childhood, and thought them beautiful but quite impractical. They prefer the worldly-wise motto: 'Trust in God, and keep your powder dry.' And they are right, as long as they want to go on living by the values of this world. These teachings of Christ are impractical for any individual who is not completely devoted to God. But if you truly seek the kingdom of heaven, then you will not care where you live, what you eat, or where you sleep. There have been men and women in past ages, and there are some today, who live in this spirit of complete dependence upon the Lord.

Some wandering monks in India take a vow not to go for alms for certain periods of time. They seat themselves in meditation, and make no attempt to provide for themselves. No one who lives that way ever starves. Several disciples of Sri Ramakrishna practised this austerity, and somehow or other they always received enough food to sustain them. The experiences of such devotees of God prove that Christ's teaching of perfect renunciation can be followed without any compromise.

Therefore take no thought, saying, What shall we eat? or, What shall we drink? or, Wherewithal shall we be clothed?

(For after all these things do the Gentiles seek:) for your heavenly Father knoweth that ye have need of all these things.

But seek ye first the kingdom of God, and his righteousness; and all these things shall be added unto you.

Sri Ramakrishna taught the same truth: 'A holy man cannot lay things up. Birds and wandering monks do not make provision for the morrow.' And he was criticized for teaching this precept to the young boys who came to him for religious instruction instead of encouraging them to live 'useful' lives in the world. He knew that all people cannot live the ideal of total renunciation, and he asked perfect self-denial only from his future message-bearers. But his householder-disciples also were expected to practise renunciation and self-surrender. He told them to fulfil their duties in the spirit of non-attachment the way a nursemaid affectionately and conscientiously takes care of her master's son but knows that he does not belong to her. And he asked them to resign themselves entirely to the will of God: 'He has placed you in the world. What can you do? Surrender yourselves to him!'

In order to illustrate the ideal of self-surrender for the householder, Sri Ramakrishna used to tell the story of a weaver who was devoted to God as Rama. The weaver was loved and trusted by everyone in his village, because he was so honest and guileless. One night he was sitting alone in the worship hall of his home when a gang of robbers arrived. They needed someone to carry their loot and took the weaver with them. After they had broken into a house and stolen many things, they piled the load on the weaver's head. Suddenly the watchman came. The robbers managed to escape, but the weaver was caught and put in jail. The next morning, the villagers unanimously told the judge that the weaver could not possibly have stolen anything. So the judge asked the weaver to describe what had happened. The weaver said: 'Your Honour, by Rama's will I was sitting in the worship hall, chanting the name of God. By Rama's will a band of robbers passed by and took me with them. By Rama's will they committed a robbery and made me carry their loot. By Rama's will the watchman arrived, and I was caught and put in jail. And by Rama's will, this morning I have been brought before your Honour.' The judge was convinced of the weaver's truthfulness and piety, and released him. On the way home, the weaver told the villagers: 'By Rama's will I have been released.'

When an individual reaches such a state of complete self-surrender to divine providence, God guides his every step. The avatars testify to this truth. Christ promises that the heavenly Father will take care of the needs of his devotee. Similarly, Sri Krishna declares in the Gita:

'. . . if a man will worship me, and meditate upon me with an undistracted mind, devoting every moment to me, I shall supply all his needs, and protect his possessions from loss.'

If we really seek the kingdom of God to the exclusion of everything else, we will feel God's grace in a special way.

'. . . and all these things shall be added unto you.' This passage has been interpreted to mean that love for God will bring material benefits. It is perfectly true that the Lord watches over his devotee and provides his necessities of life. But to worship God in order to obtain fulfilment of material desires is to use him as the means for a worldly end. It is a degeneration of religion. What is added unto the man who depends entirely on God? Spiritual benefits: purity, divine love, and eternal joy.

Take therefore no thought for the morrow: for the morrow shall take thought for the things of itself. Sufficient unto the day is the evil thereof.

How concerned we are about the future! We suffer needlessly, recalling past pain and fearing repeated hardship to come. Christ admonishes us to give up worrying. Worrying does not solve our problems; rather, it keeps the mind restless and distracted, unable to think of God. In the words of Swami Vivekananda: 'Every time we are anxious or depressed we become atheists.' But if, instead of worrying about tomorrow, we practise directing the mind to God, our problems will be solved. We will find strength and peace of mind. We will gain poise in the midst of the opposites of life. And we will eventually become spiritually illumined.

The Gita says:

> That serene one
> Absorbed in the Atman
> Masters his will,
> He knows no disquiet
> In pain or in pleasure,
> In honour, dishonour.

This serenity is not what we ordinarily think of as stoic resignation to suffering and misery. Like all embodied beings, the man of God feels heat and cold; he experiences pleasure and pain, praise and blame. But these dualities of life no longer affect him. Once he has become spiritually illumined, he recognizes that body and mind are separate from the Atman, his true Self; and his purified heart experiences the infinite happiness which exists beyond the grasp of the senses.

CHAPTER VII

Strait is the Gate

MATTHEW 7:1-29

Judge not, that ye be not judged.

For with what judgment ye judge, ye shall be judged: and with what measure ye mete, it shall be measured to you again.

And why beholdest thou the mote that is in thy brother's eye, but considerest not the beam that is in thine own eye?

Or how wilt thou say to thy brother, Let me pull out the mote out of thine eye; and, behold, a beam is in thine own eye?

ALMOST everyone has a tendency to gossip, to criticize and judge others. We relish gossiping and criticizing others because it swells our own sense of ego. Behind our criticism is the feeling: 'I don't have this weakness. I am greater than they are.' Usually, the weaknesses we seem to see in another person exist only in our own impure imagination. How many of us can really look into the depths of another human being and see all the motives which are prompting him to act in a particular way? Yet we are eager to judge and impute motives —evil motives!

Gossip may seem very innocent, yet it causes immense harm in human society, and particularly to those who indulge in it. Those who dwell on the faults of others develop the same faults themselves; for in the mind of every individual both good and bad impressions and tendencies are stored up, and if you criticize another person for a certain fault, and go on criticizing, similar tendencies which were dormant in your own subconscious mind are released and become active. If, on the other hand, you make a habit of seeing the good in others, your own good tendencies are released and strengthened. So for his own sake as well as for the sake of others, the spiritual seeker must not criticize, gossip, or judge. 'If you want peace of mind, do not find fault with others,' taught Sri Sarada Devi, a great woman saint of Bengal. 'Learn to make the whole world your own. No one is a stranger; this whole world is yours.'

In India we have a saying that the fly sits on the filth as well as on the honey, but that the bee seeks only the honey and avoids the filth. And so one of the first vows given to the religious aspirant is: 'May I follow the example of the bee, not that of the fly!' As we progress in spiritual life, we learn to see the good in everyone, we learn to have love, sympathy, and compassion for all. Real holy men have that attitude towards mankind: if you have the least drop of goodness in you, they see an ocean of goodness within that drop—not because they are overly optimistic, but because they see the possibility of future growth, and they emphasize it. They know that through the grace of God a man may be freed in one moment from all sin and bondage. Swami Brahmananda used to say:

'Heaps of cotton can be burnt with one matchstick; similarly, one gracious glance from God can wipe out mountains of sins. The man who appears as a sinner today may be a saint to-morrow.'

Does this mean that we should be blind to one another's faults, and never try to correct them? No, Jesus does not say that. But he says:

Thou hypocrite, first cast out the beam out of thine own eye; and then shalt thou see clearly to cast out the mote out of thy brother's eye.

Jesus is asking us to correct our own defects before we try to correct our brother's. We are hypocrites as long as we rationalize our weaknesses and find them worthy of forgiveness, yet remain unwilling to bear with our brother's imperfections. When we have cast the beam out of our own eyes, when our hearts are purified and we really have love for mankind, then we can tell others where they fail—not with malicious relish, but with sympathy and compassion. My master, like all such great souls, had moods when he saw no faults in anyone. He saw God everywhere, and nothing but God. But at other times he scolded us, thundered at us, pounded at our faults. Afterwards he would say: 'Do you think you can run away from me, because I am apparently so cruel? The mother holds the child, and spanks it. The child cries "Mother!" And all the while it is in its mother's arms.' But until we feel such love ourselves, we have no right to criticize others. Hands off! We will find it more profitable to see the fault in ourselves.

Give not that which is holy unto the dogs, neither cast ye your pearls before swine, lest they trample them under their feet, and turn again and rend you.

Here Jesus tells his apostles how they are to teach the truth of God. He warns them to discriminate, to preach only to those who are prepared to receive and follow the teaching. We find parallel passages in the scriptures of Vedanta. In the Mundaka Upanishad we read: 'Let the truth of Brahman be taught only to those who obey his law, who are devoted to him, and who are pure in heart.' Similarly, after giving the message of the Gita to Arjuna, Sri Krishna says: 'You must never tell this holy truth to anyone who lacks self-control and devotion, or who despises his teacher and mocks at me.'

A real guru does not entrust an exalted precept to an unspiritual man, who may misinterpret it, misuse it to justify his worldly cravings, or ridicule it. There are certain conditions which an individual must meet before he can assimilate religious truth. He must have purity, a thirst for divine knowledge, and perseverance. When both the aspirant and his teacher are properly qualified, spiritual life becomes fruitful.

The Upanishads tell us that many persons, though they hear of the Self, do not understand it.

'Wonderful is he who speaks of it. Intelligent is he who learns of it. Blessed is he who, taught by a good teacher, is able to understand it.'

Ask, and it shall be given you; seek, and ye shall find; knock, and it shall be opened unto you:
For every one that asketh receiveth; and he that seeketh findeth; and to him that knocketh it shall be opened.
Or what man is there of you, whom if his son ask bread, will he give him a stone?
Or if he ask a fish, will he give him a serpent?

In this passage Jesus sums up the whole truth of religion. Before the door to the kingdom of God is opened, the spiritual aspirant must have both longing for God and faith.

What is faith? It is *knowing* that when we knock at the door it will be opened. This faith does not come until we have achieved purity of heart. Lusts, passions, and fleshly desires prevent us from seeing God, who is nevertheless present at all times, everywhere. The more we knock, the more we ask and pray, the more this world will be seen to be a mere appearance, and the reality of God's presence will open to us.

True longing for God—the hungering and mourning which Jesus calls blessed—comes only when we are no longer attached to the objects of this world. We must reach a stage of spiritual unfoldment in which, in the words of the Psalmist, the soul yearns for divine union 'as the hart panteth after the water brooks'. The great Hindu mystic Chaitanya longed for the vision of Krishna so desperately that an instant's separation from his beloved Lord seemed to him like a thousand years. He felt that his heart would burn away with its desire and that the world, without God, was 'a heartless void'. When this intensity of longing arises, God grants the prayer of his devotee.

If ye then, being evil, know how to give good gifts unto your children, how much more shall your Father which is in heaven give good things to them that ask him?

We must always remember that God loves us, who are his own children, and that we have a right to his indulgence. Sri Ramakrishna said:

'If a son begs continually for his share of the property, his parents will give it to him even before he comes of age. The Lord will surely answer your prayers if you feel restless for him. He is our own Father and Mother. We have every right to claim our inheritance from him.'

Therefore all things whatsoever ye would that men should do to you, do ye even so to them: for this is the law and the prophets.

The truth which Jesus teaches here is common to all the major religions. It is the Golden Rule, our guide for conduct in human society. There are almost identical passages in the Mahabharata, the famous Indian epic: 'Treat others as thou wouldst thyself be treated.' 'Do nothing to thy neighbour which hereafter thou wouldst not have thy neighbour do to thee.' Our goal in life is to experience union with God and all beings. We can make this end the means of realizing God. If we practise trying to see the unity, if we do unto others as we would have them do unto us, our consciousness will eventually be transformed. Then we will actually see the one God vibrating in every atom of the universe, and love him in all beings.

Teaching Arjuna the truth of universal love, Sri Krishna says:

> Who burns with the bliss
> And suffers the sorrow
> Of every creature
> Within his own heart,

Making his own
Each bliss and each sorrow:
Him I hold highest
Of all the yogis.

There are some who believe that the search for God is apt to
make the searcher indifferent to the sufferings of others, but
the very opposite is true. The more we turn to God with love,
the more sensitive we become to the problems of others and
the more we care for them. We begin to realize that our own
Self is the Self in everyone else. Because we wish to be happy,
we cannot cause unhappiness to others; and so we cannot hurt
others in any way. My master used to say: 'Go and meditate,
chant the Lord's name. Then you will find your heart expand-
ing in sympathy for all.'

*Enter ye in at the strait gate: for wide is the gate, and broad
is the way, that leadeth to destruction, and many there be
which go in thereat:*
*Because strait is the gate, and narrow is the way, which
leadeth unto life, and few there be that find it.*

Jesus warns us that realization of God is not easy. Purity of
heart can only be achieved after a great struggle. In the Katha
Upanishad we read: 'Like the sharp edge of a razor, the sages
say, is the path. Narrow it is, and difficult to tread!' We are
also told that the Lord created the senses outgoing:

'Accordingly, man looks towards what is without, and sees not
what is within. Rare is he who, longing for immortality, shuts
his eyes to what is without and beholds the Self.'

The natural human tendency is to rush out through the broad
ways of the senses and lose oneself in the world. The process
of religious growth is to turn that whole current of life around
and make it flow inward, through 'the strait gate'.
    The meaning of the 'strait gate' seems to be made quite clear

by the Yoga teachings on spiritual awakening. The yogis of
India identify three nerve-passages in the spine, which are
called the ida, the pingala, and the sushumna. The ida and the
pingala are the two outer passages of the spinal nerves, but
modern anatomists have been unable to find any use for the
sushumna, the central passage. Yoga, however, reveals its use.
According to Yoga there are seven centres of spiritual consciousness located along the spine in the human body. At the
base of the spine a reserve of latent spiritual energy is situated
which, awakened by spiritual practices and devotion to God,
flows upward through the narrow channel of the sushumna.
As this energy reaches the higher centres of consciousness, it
produces various degrees of enlightenment.

As long as the mind is attached to worldliness consciousness
dwells in the three lower centres, at the organs of evacuation
and reproduction, and at the navel. The mind then contains
no spiritual ideals or pure thoughts. The fourth centre of consciousness is in the heart region. When the spiritual energy
rises to this centre, the aspirant sees a divine light and experiences ecstasy. As the energy reaches the fifth centre, at the
throat, he wants to think and talk only of God. At the sixth
centre, between the eyebrows, he experiences the vision of
God. There is still a slight sense of ego left, and the aspirant
longs to break down that last barrier of separation from God.
When the spiritual energy bursts into the highest centre, in
the brain, the realization dawns that 'I and my Father are one',
and perfect divine union is attained. So the sushumna would
be literally a narrow gate leading to eternal life, to the knowledge of God himself.

In India, Yoga teachings on the spiritual centres have been
corroborated by the experiences of aspirants for thousands of
years. But mystical realization is, of course, not limited to
India—it is the same for all, whether they are Hindus,
Christians, Jews, or followers of any other religious path. For
a striking resemblance to the experiences of the Indian yogis,
consider the example of Jacob Boehme, a Christian mystic of

the sixteenth century, who describes in his *Confessions* his own spiritual awakening:

'For the Holy Ghost will not be held in the sinful flesh, but rises up like a lightning-flash, as fire sparkles and flashes out of a stone when a man strikes it.

'But when the flash is caught in the fountain of the heart, then the Holy Spirit rises up, in the seven unfolding fountain spirits, into the brain, like the dawning of the day, the morning redness. . . .

'From this God I take my knowledge and from no other thing; neither will I know any other thing than that same God. . . .

'Though an angel from heaven should tell this to me, yet for all that I could not believe it, much less lay hold on it; for I should always doubt whether it was certainly so or no. But the Sun itself arises in my spirit, and therefore I am most sure of it.'

Beware of false prophets, which come to you in sheep's clothing, but inwardly they are ravening wolves.
Ye shall know them by their fruits. Do men gather grapes of thorns, or figs of thistles?
Even so every good tree bringeth forth good fruit; but a corrupt tree bringeth forth evil fruit.
A good tree cannot bring forth evil fruit, neither can a corrupt tree bring forth good fruit.
Every tree that bringeth not forth good fruit is hewn down, and cast into the fire.
Wherefore by their fruits ye shall know them.

Jesus tells us to discriminate between true and false prophets and true and false religion. True religion shows us how to overcome the world and attain the knowledge of God, but the teachers of false religion hold out the promise of success and wealth in the world. The fruits of true religion are illumination, selfless love, and compassion for all. Sri Ramakrishna followed the paths of many religions during his life on earth, and always applied the same test to each: 'Will it give me the illumination of God?' When told about some new sect, he would ask: 'Does it teach love for God? Does it teach people how to realize God?' If not, he would have nothing to do with it.

A religious leader should be an illumined soul. If he teaches the knowledge of God without having that knowledge himself, he is like the blind leading the blind. But it is difficult for a spiritual aspirant to judge the fitness of a teacher or prophet, because a truly religious man does not advertise his holiness. There are, however, certain qualities which are characteristic of a genuine spiritual leader. First, he knows the spirit of the scriptures. Second, he is sinless and pure in heart, which means that he lives what he preaches—an intellectual grasp of religious truth is not enough. Third, he works out of pure love for mankind; he does not teach with any ulterior motive—such as the desire for wealth or fame. The spiritual leader or prophet who possesses these three qualities can be trusted, and the aspirant who approaches him with humility and reverence is blessed.

Not every one that saith unto me, Lord, Lord, shall enter into the kingdom of heaven; but he that doeth the will of my Father which is in heaven.

Many will say to me in that day, Lord, Lord, have we not prophesied in thy name? and in thy name have cast out devils? and in thy name done many wonderful works?

And then will I profess unto them, I never knew you: depart from me, ye that work iniquity.

These verses have frequently been used to justify a kind of humanistic religion. The humanists interpret the phrase about doing 'the will of my Father' as a command to perform good works in the external world. They say, 'Lord, Lord', to give the work a touch of emotion, and then go ahead with their social service. They use God as a scavenger to clean out the drains of human society.

But there is only one way of doing the will of God, and that is, first, to realize him. Until we have done that, we can never know what his will is. This does not mean that we must give up our humanitarian work. If a man is hungry, feed him; if he is sick, nurse him. However, we must do this, not as philanthropy or service to mankind, but as service to God out of love for God.

There is a very important distinction between the two attitudes of philanthropy and service to God. Among those who set out to serve mankind we often find egotism arising. They survey their work, and soon they are saying: 'Without me, everything will go to pieces. Nothing must stand in the way of this work. The world needs me.' And then, it is not long before they are saying: 'God needs me.' When I first came to this country, I visited a Sunday-school class—the teacher had written on the board: 'God needs your help.' Later on I heard a minister say: 'We all know that God is not omnipotent. We must help him to gain more power.' That is the direct opposite of what Jesus taught. Jesus taught that God does not need us; we need him. He taught that the wonderful works we do in the name of God will not enable us to enter into the kingdom of heaven; we work 'iniquity' unless we surrender our egos to God and merge our wills in his will.

Regarding selfless service, Swami Vivekananda said:

'It is sheer nonsense on the part of any man to think that he is born to help the world. It is simply vanity; it is selfishness insinuating itself in the form of virtue. . . .

'The desire to do good is the highest motive power we have if we know that it is a privilege to help others. Do not stand on a high pedestal and take five cents in your hand and say, "Here, my poor man!" But be grateful that the poor man is there, so that by making a gift to him you are able to help yourself. It is not the receiver that is blessed, but it is the giver. . . . What can we do at best? Build a hospital, make

roads, or erect charity asylums. . . . One volcanic eruption may
sweep away all our roads and hospitals and cities and buildings.

'Let us give up all this foolish talk of doing good to the
world. It is not waiting for your or my help. Yet we must work
and constantly do good, because it is a blessing to ourselves.
That is the only way we can become perfect. . . . We think that
we have helped some man and expect him to thank us; and
because he does not, unhappiness comes to us. Why should we
expect anything in return for what we do? Be grateful to the
man you help, think of him as God. Is it not a great privilege
to be allowed to worship God by helping our fellow man?

'Do what good you can, some evil will inhere in it; but do
all without regard to personal result. Give up all results to the
Lord, then neither good nor evil will affect you.'

Religion must be neither egocentric nor altruistic, but theo-
centric. We must centre our whole mind upon God, and then,
extending our arms to everyone, embrace all in the love of God.

*Therefore whosoever heareth these sayings of mine, and
doeth them, I will liken him unto a wise man, which built his
house upon a rock:*

*And the rain descended, and the floods came, and the winds
blew, and beat upon that house; and it fell not: for it was
founded upon a rock.*

*And every one that heareth these sayings of mine, and doeth
them not, shall be likened unto a foolish man, which built his
house upon the sand:*

*And the rain descended, and the floods came, and the winds
blew, and beat upon that house; and it fell: and great was the
fall of it.*

The rock upon which the wise man builds his house is the
rock of spiritual experience. When once you have been face
to face with Reality, when you stand upon that, then nothing
can shake you. Until we have built upon that rock—no matter
how strong our faith may seem to be emotionally—we shall

be shaken by the storms of doubt; and the house will fall, and have to be rebuilt again and again.

A Christ, a Buddha, a Ramakrishna arises and says, 'I have seen Him!' No second-hand report, no amount of study, no wealth of eloquence can be compared to the absolute guarantee of first-hand witness which such an illumined teacher brings us. But even the testimony of these illumined teachers, even that is not enough—their testimony must move us to action. The faith of a person who merely says, 'I believe in Jesus', or 'I accept Buddha', and does nothing further, is not true faith. 'And every one that heareth these sayings of mine, and doeth them not, shall be likened unto a foolish man, which built his house upon the sand.' True faith makes us strive until we too are reborn in spirit and enter into the kingdom of heaven.

Actually to have been present, to listen to the Sermon on the Mount, must have been one of the most tremendous experiences a human being could have—yet even this was an experience at second-hand; and so we find that some of Christ's most intimate disciples were later troubled with doubts. Swami Vivekananda had doubts too, even after long intimacy with Sri Ramakrishna; and those doubts only vanished finally when he directly perceived the truth of God. And so we return to the basic principle that religion is something we ourselves have to do, and be, and live—or else it is nothing.

And it came to pass, when Jesus had ended these sayings, the people were astonished at his doctrine:

For he taught them as one having authority, and not as the scribes.

I would like to quote a passage from Swami Vivekananda's lecture on Christ: 'He had no other occupation in life, no other thought except that one, that he was Spirit. He was disembodied, unfettered, unbound Spirit. And not only so, but he, with his marvellous vision, had found that every man and woman, whether Jew or Gentile, whether rich or poor, whether saint or sinner, was the embodiment of the same undying

Spirit as himself. Therefore, the one work his whole life showed was calling them to realize their own spiritual nature. Give up, he said, these superstitious dreams that you are low and that you are poor. Think not that you are trampled upon and tyrannized over as if you were slaves, for within you is something that can never be tyrannized over, never be trampled upon, never be troubled, never be killed. Know, he declared, "the kingdom of God is within you." You are all Sons of God, immortal Spirit. Dare you stand up and say, not only that 'I am the Son of God" but I shall also find in my heart of hearts that "I and my Father are one".'

This is the eternal gospel which every great Messenger has taught and which Christ asks all of us who would be his children first to hear, then to realize for ourselves.